THE ADVENTURES OF RIVERBOAT JOHN

THE ADVENTURES OF RIVERBOAT JOHN

GLIMPSES OF HUNTSVILLE
in the 1950s

"RIVERBOAT JOHN" FERGUSON

THE
History
PRESS

Published by The History Press
Charleston, SC 29403
www.historypress.net

First published 2009

ISBN 978.1.5402.2375.3

Library of Congress Cataloging-in-Publication Data

Ferguson, John (John Edwin), 1942-
The adventures of Riverboat John : glimpses of Huntsville in the 1950s / John Ferguson.
p. cm.
ISBN 978-1-5402-2375-.
1. Ferguson, John (John Edwin), 1942---Childhood and youth--Anecdotes. 2. Huntsville
(Ala.)--Social life and customs--20th century--Anecdotes. I. Title.
F334.H9F47 2009
976.1'97--dc22
2009038809

CONTENTS

CONTENTS

INTRODUCTION

T hese stories are merely brief glances, peeks and snippets of some of the things I saw, heard or remember as a boy growing up in Huntsville, Alabama. They are my stories and my observations and are not intended to be the final word but rather glimpses only.

Growing up in Huntsville in the '50s was quite an experience. The '40s featured the end of the Great Depression for many in the South. The end of World War II and the return of the soldier brought a new sense of patriotism, freedom and prosperity to our country.

In 1950, our country entered the space age when Werner von Braun and the German rocket team came to Huntsville. Our city, with its agricultural economy, was transformed overnight.

Most of the things I talk about in this book happened in or near or are connected to Huntsville during the 1950s. I have not attempted to put anyone "on the spot" or to embarrass anyone, including myself. It is my hope

The old courthouse.

Summer 1958, Space Capital of the Universe.

that this book will inspire others to tell their stories and create conversation about the 1950s. Everyone has a story or two to tell.

> *They say you can't go down that road that you left on when you left home,*
> *but I went back home.*
> *I have climbed the highest mountains. I have sailed the Seven Seas.*
> *I have hiked a hundred highways. I have smelled the desert breeze, and I*
> *went back home.*

I wrote this song in 1993 after thinking about how hard it is for many to go back home. I always enjoy going back home and visiting friends and memories. I enjoy reminiscing and I hope you will, too.

SATURDAY MORNING IN TOWN

"Fifty cents in my pocket"

Growing up in the '40s and '50s, there was always something interesting to do in Huntsville, Alabama. It was a period of imagination spurred on by literature (lots of good books) and, for most of us, very little spending money.

There was more leisure time and more spending money than in the generation before World War II. Most kids had their chores to do, and at our home we always had some kind of work to do on Saturday morning. It was digging, painting, carpentry work, cleaning, repair or something like that. We always got up on Saturday morning as early as possible and got whatever had to be done completed in a speedy manner. When Dad and Mom were satisfied, we lit out for town.

Huntsville on Saturday was chock-full with every kind of conveyance (wagons, cars, trucks, bicycles, motorcycles, scooters and more). People everywhere were standing around talking, trading, visiting, whittling and doing other activities that humans do.

A lot of people smoked back then. It was fashionable to smoke. Men smoked their pipes and cigars, chewed tobacco and dipped snuff. Some of the ladies dipped snuff and smoked in public. Women didn't wear pantsuits or jeans to town back then. A lot of the men wore bib overalls.

You had to be careful when you were a kid walking around with men dipping and chewing. You had to be a good dodger of a quick tobacco spit, or you might end up with spit in your eye or on your best shirt. If you were

Folks gathered around the courthouse.

Sesquicentennial Parade, 1955.

barefoot, you had to be careful where you walked unless you wanted a chewy-gooey foot.

The main target for me on Saturday morning was either the Lyric Theatre or the Grande Theatre. There was a lot to see and do first before going to the theatre.

First was a trip to the library. The Madison County Library was one of the original Carnegie libraries. It had a pretty good selection of classic books, magazines, reference books and more. I would always check one book out every week after returning the one I had read.

My favorite authors were Mark Twain, Robert Louis Stevenson, Jack London, Jules Verne, Charles Dickens and Herman Melville—books of adventure, travel and imagination. We had to wear a shirt and our shoes to go in the library. Sometimes we would sit and listen to a story being read during story time. Then it was off to explore the stores.

A trip to the old hardware downtown was a treat. It had every kind of gizmo of the day plus a lot of things from times past. Then there was the regular hardware, Hopper Hardware. Mike Hopper and I were in the same class at Huntsville High. Plowshares, cast-iron pots, stoves, heaters, tools, hardware, nuts, bolts and more. Then it was once around the big furniture store and a trip or two to the clothing stores.

Dunnavants, Belks, Montgomery Ward and the dime stores. Everything from soup to nuts for a little boy to look over until you got that look from the proprietor that it was time to move on. Now, if you were lucky, you had a half of a dollar in your pocket. That meant you could do a lot more than just get in the movies. You could buy a big old ice cream cone at Tom Dark's City Drugstore and read all the magazines that had just come out. Two big scoops of real ice cream for a nickel.

Or you might buy a couple of hamburgers from the Snow White on the Square or a hamburger at Wimpy's Grill. Wimpy's had a pool hall in the back. We would always try to go back there and watch the men shoot pool. Most of the time we were told to leave, but the chance to slip in every once in a while was worth all the effort. Wimpy's was kind of special because they did have a good hamburger. They precooked them and kept them in a big pan of hot water next to the grill. They were absolutely delicious.

My friend Andy Roberts, who is now a very successful and respected attorney in Huntsville, worked there while he was going to school. It was owned by Mr.

East Side Square storefronts, Wimpy's.

Snow White Northside Square.

Lones and Mr. Mullins. The name of the restaurant came from the cartoon character Popeye. The flickering sign out front showed the character Wimpy eating a hamburger, which he was always doing in the cartoon.

By the way, I am proud of Andy. I never heard him curse or tell an off-color story. Besides working at Wimpy's, he had a job at Madison Street Market. He delivered coal and groceries to the neighboring houses. His transportation was a bicycle with a large wheel on the rear and a small one on the front with a basket located above to carry the product. He graduated from Auburn and worked for Brown Engineering for a while and then went back to college and got a law degree. That is a long way from sweeping floors in a poolroom.

Another big event downtown was the street celebration when the United States successfully launched the Explorer I satellite into space. It was February 1, 1958. The Soviets had put up the first satellite on October 4, 1957. Our country needed to celebrate. We were especially proud because Redstone Arsenal was directly involved in the program.

People began to congregate on the courthouse square just about dark. A lot of people were shooting fireworks. Some people were even shooting shotguns and pistols to celebrate. The most dramatic thing was a stick of dynamite. I think it was taken (stolen) from Hopper Hardware. It left a huge hole in the street, and we all ran away from it as fast as we could because we knew someone was going to get into trouble. No one got caught.

When you were downtown you might have gotten a bag of popcorn as long as your arm from the Dime store. You could smell it all over town.

Uncle Sam's Pawnshop was a must for me. I just had to look at all the knives, army surplus, watches, guns and other items. Then it was time to go to the movies. Usually I went to the Lyric Theatre because it always seemed to have the best westerns. My hero was Gene Autry. My best memories were watching Gene and the other cowboys while eating Milk Duds alongside a bag of popcorn and a wax cup with two cubes of ice and Coca-Cola. The Lone Ranger and his friend Tonto were also favorites.

After watching the movie, weekly newsreel and the weekly serial (*Flash Gordon*, *Superman* and others), we were tired and ready to head back home. The manager had a diplomatic way of telling us that our time was up. He would turn on his flashlight and point at the exit.

Out of the exit and once more around the dwindling crowd at the square, we hoofed it home. If we had fifty cents to spend, we had a full day. If we just had enough to get in the movie, we were still happy. There was nothing like Saturday morning in town.

COTTON ON THE CANAL

"Exploring the Big Spring Canal"

The west side of the square of the Madison County Courthouse in Huntsville is called "Cotton Row." That is where the cotton buyers or cotton brokers used to buy and sell cotton from the early 1800s to the turn of the century.

At one time, Madison County grew more cotton per acre than any other county in the United States. Cotton was loaded onto canal barges and shipped down the canal to the Tennessee River. Big Spring canal was located just behind Cotton Row. Its source is the Big Spring, which still gushes a lot of ice-cold water today. It is the main reason the Native Americans and, later on, settlers made use of the area. Huntsville was named after John Hunt, one of the first white settlers.

The canal was called the Fearn Canal originally and was built in 1825. It has been called the Indian Creek Canal and other names, as well. Most people do not realize that it connected with Indian Creek at Triana, Alabama, on the Tennessee River and ran all the way from downtown Huntsville across what is now Redstone Arsenal.

At first we just played in the creeks and rain-swollen ditches. We made little rafts and crude boats. We got better as time went on. You never knew how far you could go when the creeks were full. Lots of water came off Monte Sano Mountain, Huntsville Mountain and the surrounding hills.

One day we went all the way to the edge of Redstone Arsenal and could go no farther because it was a restricted area. You could see a lot of things

West Side Square Cotton Row signs.

West Side Square scene.

from the canal that you could not see from the roads above it. You could see the backs of houses, and you could find things that people had thrown away or things that had gotten caught in the ditches in the rain and washed off. We were like the pirates we had read about—sailing on the seas, or on the rivers, of yesteryear.

Many times we would pretend to be steamboating, like on the Mississippi when Mark Twain was at the wheel. We would act out or use our imaginations to pretend that we were characters like Tom Sawyer and Huckleberry Finn being pirates on the river. Sometimes we would stop along the way, build a fire and sit and jaw or go exploring.

When I finally got to be in the Explorer Scouts, we got permission to go across Redstone Arsenal to Triana in the canal. There were a lot of places that were not navigable, but in our canoes we did pretty well. I don't know what the other boys were thinking, but all the while I was traveling along I was thinking of the thousands of pounds of cotton that had gone through this canal to Triana. I thought of the thousands of fingers that were worn and tired from picking it. I thought of all the mules that had done the plowing. I thought of

Big Spring, Huntsville, 1910.

all the mule wagons and the drivers who had brought the cotton to the square and Cotton Row. There were a lot of memories and adventures.

It was spooky going across Redstone Arsenal. There were government signs and warning signs everywhere—all of those secret guided missiles and rockets and who knows what else. Barbed wire and chain-link fence and watchful eyes. No cameras allowed.

I thought about all the times that those boatmen were glad to get to Huntsville to get a load of cotton and spend some leisure time in town while they were waiting for their crafts to be loaded. I wondered what some of their pastimes might have been like, shooting pool in a saloon, getting a haircut in a tonsillitory or going to the theatre. I am sure a lot of them just stayed down on the banks and played their banjos, fiddles, guitars, whistles and a new-fangled contraption called a harmonica. I am sure that the town ladies came to visit also.

Being in Triana must have been different, too, because it was the actual river town at which the paddle-wheelers were loading or offloading. There would have been showboats with entertainment to offer with music, dancing and theatre. Might have been a little gambling going on, too.

Dr. Frances Roberts, one of my mentors growing up, told me that there were excursions on the canalboats that went to and from Triana. Dr. Roberts was a PhD and an authority on the history of Huntsville and the Tennessee Valley. I sat on her porch as many times as I could to hear about the exciting

Big Spring, Huntsville, 1915.

past. That was one way the Huntsville citizens could get to the riverboats at Triana. It was a long way by wagon.

Of course they could have taken the Whitesburg Road out to Ditto Landing, which was fourteen miles from downtown Huntsville and much closer. Ditto's Landing was an interesting place, too. Cotton was also rafted or floated down the Flint River and the Paint Rock River and loaded near Ditto's Landing at Whitesburg.

John Ditto operated a ferry there during the 1800s long before there was a bridge across the Tennessee River. During the days of the steamboats, there was a lot of activity there. Then the trains came. They changed boat traffic quite a bit. There was even a train that was hauled back and forth from Ditto Landing to Gunter's Landing in Guntersville, Alabama. It was in service until the early 1960s.

Who would believe it? Imagine seeing a train on a boat. The train traveled between Huntsville to Gadsden and back by way of Guntersville, up Sand Mountain and back down to Gadsden. Lots of crazy things happened on the river.

I'll never forget my trip and "exploring" the Big Spring Canal and my trip to Triana from the Big Spring behind Cotton Row across Redstone Arsenal in a canoe. And I'll never forget all those "cotton pickers," pirates, raftsmen and steamboaters.

DRIVE-IN MOVIE THEATRES
IN HUNTSVILLE

*"Plenty to do but not a lot
of money to spend"*

We had three main drive-in movie theatres in Huntsville during the 1950s. Woody's Drive-in out on the north end of town, and the Whitesburg Drive-in on the south end of town. We also had the combination of the Parkway Drive-in and the 231 Drive-in. The Whitesburg Drive-in opened in 1949 and closed in 1979. It had four hundred car spaces.

Woody's opened in 1951 and closed in 1976. The Parkway Drive-in opened in 1955. It was advertised as the "world's largest screen and drive-in cafeteria" and had 660 car spaces. The screen was advertised as being five stories high, and a large fireworks display occurred on opening night. The theatre joined with the 231 Drive-in (which opened on April 3, 1953) on a fifteen-acre site located between the Parkway and U.S. 231.

Starting May 1, 1955, the ads for the 231 Drive-in noted the following: "You can step over to the new Parkway Theatre and hear Slim Lay and the [WHBS] Homefolks tonight. Appearing nightly at intermission." The first section next to the Parkway had spaces for 660 cars, with the second screen being located next to U.S. 231.

There was a drive-in on Highway 72 West called the Highway 72 Drive-in. It opened in 1960 and closed in 1979. It was torn down to build an office park. It had about four hundred car slots.

Memorial Parkway.

There was a drive-in called the Regal in the early 1950s that catered to the black population of the Huntsville area. The Princess Theatre was downtown, and it was a walk-in catering solely to African Americans. Segregation was still very much in full force then. As a young man, I never thought about what black folks did when I didn't see them working or doing their jobs.

In 1958, there were about one hundred drive-in movies across the state of Alabama. In 2008, there were fewer than ten. A drive-in movie was set up for people to watch movies through the windshields of their automobiles. Speakers were mounted on poles about four feet high, and they attached to your car window, which could be partially opened or closed. There was a volume adjustment on each speaker. Sometimes people would forget to place the speaker back on the holder, and they would drive off with the speaker still in the car after ripping the wire out of the pole.

Drive-ins also catered to families. Mom and Dad always liked the Whitesburg Drive-in best. There was a playground at our drive-ins right under the huge screen on which the movies were projected. There were also chairs for folks who wanted to sit there and watch both the movie and their children play.

The snack bar at a drive-in sold all kinds of interesting food: snow cones, hot dogs and chili dogs, hamburgers and cheeseburgers, barbecue, French fries, onion rings, pizza, popcorn, colas, peanuts, milkshakes and candy. Drive-ins were always having promotions. Sometimes you could get in for one dollar for a full carload.

Glimpses of Huntsville in the 1950s

When the Whitesburg Drive-in opened, the price was forty cents for adults and ten cents for children over five, and children under five got in free.

For several years in a row, the Parkway/231 Drive-in had a Big John contest night. They always showed a John Wayne movie when they had the contest. The song "Big John" by the singer Jimmy Dean was very popular. At the intermission they turned the lights on over the concession stand, and the emcee (Slim Lay) held the contest. If your name was John you could enter the contest. Whoever was the biggest won the prize.

I won the contest one night. My prize was one night's free admission to the drive-in and a case of twenty-four Coca-Cola drinks in a wooden drink pallet. I don't mind telling you that the main reason I won was because it was a big football night and it was misting rain. A case of Coca-Colas and another free admission on any night I chose was a good prize for a boy with very little spending money.

I didn't own a car and my father would not let us drive his car. Unless we went to the drive-in with Mom and Dad, we had to buddy up with a friend who got a carload of guys without dates together. It was easy for a bunch of guys to get into trouble when a crowd was out carousing in a car.

The best way to go if you didn't have a car was on a double-date. Plenty of smooching going on. This meant that you had to have money to get in the movies and buy your date a cold drink, snacks and more. I can tell you, this didn't happen very often for me.

Another point about the '50s was the way pornography was handled. One of the drive-ins had a late-night series called "Nurse-A-Rama." It was intended for adults and was considered to be risqué or pornographic at the time. The movies would start out at a late hour and last all night long. The series involved nurses and their escapades. They progressively became more risqué as the night went on. The more you watched the worse (or better) it got, depending on your expectations. These movies would be considered mild today, but at the time were vulgar in the eyes of the majority of the public.

Television ruined the drive-in business. People started building dens in their new homes and making the television the center of attraction. It cost a whole lot less to operate than going to the movies.

"Plenty to do but not a lot of money to spend."

MUSSEL BOAT CAMPS

"Sadie was a good old gal."

Fifteen years old, no car, no money and no girlfriend. Wow! Who is that pretty little girl getting off the bus the first day of school? I wanted to know. I followed her to class. She was in the homeroom right next to mine.

I was in love. Blonde hair, blue eyes and cute as a button. But what good was all that? Who would want to "go out" with someone like me? Go out! How can you go out if you don't have a way to go or the money to spend when you get there? I watched her get on that bus after school was out. Wow! What a pretty girl.

Wonder if she would even notice me if I walked up to her and said hello. I thought about her all that evening and up into the night. I wonder where she lives. She rides the bus. I'll bet she lives out in the country.

I did find out her name was Sadie. My mother's name was Sadie.

After I got up enough courage, I got on the same bus she came in on every day and rode to the end of the line. I knew some kids who lived there, and I asked the bus driver if it was okay. I wanted to find out where she lived. When the bus got down near the river, she got off and disappeared down the road in no time. I got off as soon as the bus stopped again and started walking back down the long river road to where the bus had stopped before when she got off. I tried to hide my actions so no one would know what I was up to.

East Clinton May Festival.

I discovered that Sadie lived in a mussel boat camp in an old bus that was up off the ground on six feet of blocks. The place stunk to high heaven with dead mussels and mussel shells. There must have been ten old thirty-foot-long plywood boats with racks full of mussel chain hooks. It was all curious to me.

Sadie and her family lived in that old bus. It was hand painted crudely with silver and had a tarpaulin extended over the top and out front for an awning. An old gasoline-operated wringer washer set next to a big wash pot stand. There was a big tumbler used to drop the mussel meat out of the shells after they had been cooked in a big cauldron.

I walked into the camp. Sadie was nowhere to be seen, but her father and a couple of other men were working with the mussels they had brought in that day. They brought in over one thousand pounds each day in the thirty-foot boats. I was curious. They wanted to know what I was doing there and who I was.

I told them I went to school with Sadie and that I was just out looking for arrowheads on the river. They must have liked me because they started telling me all about mussel boats and how to work mussels. I didn't realize how much work there was to mussel harvesting.

Sadie's father reminded me of one of those mountain "moonshiners" you see in the movies. But he was real nice. He called his daughter out of the "bus" house to let her know that I was there. Sadie was surprised to see me but acted like she was ashamed of where she lived. I didn't let on like I cared. I met her mom, who was beginning to wash clothes.

Sadie told me she only had two dresses and that her mom washed, starched and ironed them so that she would not have to wear the same one two days in a row. She told me that she got off the bus a long way down the road from where the mussel boat camp was so that the other kids would not make fun of her. She made me promise not to tell the others and not to make fun of her "home." She said they had moved around a lot on the rivers, especially the Tennessee River.

Mussels were used to make buttons and other mother-of-pearl items, and they were very much in demand. Her dad let me go out and work on the boats with them numerous times after that, and I learned a lot about collecting mussels. The boats were dragged behind a canvas underwater sail bag and drifted side by side with the current. They could drag in over three hundred pounds of mussels in one haul, and the boats could hold about five or six hauls.

The mussels grabbed on to chains with metal hooks on the end and were on frames. This was lots of work. Sadie said that it was a way of life. Her dad had high hopes for her. He wanted her to get an education so she could have a better life than that of living in mussel camps. This way of life was going to be a thing of the past one day. He said that his family had been "river rats" all their lives, all the way back in his family as far as anyone could remember. He told me that the Indians harvested mussels from the rivers centuries ago and used the shells for tools and the mussel meat for food. He claimed his family had Native American blood in them, probably Cherokee.

Sadie and I got to be friends that year. I didn't need a car to "take her out" or any money. All I had to do was ride the bus home with her after school. It was always a long walk back home, but someone usually stopped and gave me a ride.

I visited the camp many times and enjoyed being with the "river people" every chance I got. My romantic ideas about Sadie disappeared when she ran off at age fifteen with a grown man from the cotton mill. I will always have fond memories of her and her family and the knowledge gained from them about mussel boats and mussel camps.

I stayed in touch with her father for several years and would call on them often. They were always nice to me and always seemed glad to see me.

Sadie's name was never mentioned because it really hurt her father. The last time I saw him before I heard he died was at a mussel camp and sales point near Triana, on Indian Creek on the Tennessee River.

Years later, while in line at the Madison County Courthouse waiting for my automobile license tag, I had a conversation with an older lady in line. It was Sadie. Her hair was no longer blonde. Her beautiful face and smile were old. Her jaws sank in from lack of dental care. She was stooped over slightly. She said hello to me and said that I looked familiar. We hugged. After all these years, three husbands, several children, grand-children and a life of labor, here she was.

We both talked about all the things that happened to us. We talked about her dad and mom. We talked about the mussel boats and mussel camps—about how it had all died out and was now a "way of the past" and about how now people were diving for mussels and sending them to Japan to make cultured pearls.

One thing stayed the same: those beautiful blue eyes. Sadie was a good old gal.

I ALWAYS WANTED TO
BE A COWBOY

"Don't say nuthin' bad about Gene Autry!"

As a little boy growing up in the '40s and '50s after the end of World War II, I had my heroes. My main heroes were my Dad and the cowboys who appeared on the silver screen.

The biggest and best cowboy hero was Gene Autry. If we could, we went to the Lyric, Grand or Center Theatres in Huntsville on Saturday mornings. Gene Autry was a real cowboy who was born on a ranch in Texas. He was raised on a ranch in Oklahoma and worked as a telegraph operator for the railroad before being discovered by the great American humorist, Will Rogers. My hero's voice sounded like that of Jimmie Rodgers, the very popular country singer. Autry was also a pilot during World War II. He stopped making movies, which earned him $1 million per year, to fly planes in combat in the U.S. Army Air Corps for $85 per month. I never saw Gene Autry do or say anything wrong. I wore my blue jeans rolled up just like he did. We called it a "Gene Autry" roll.

I never had the boots or hats or fancy guns, but I did end up with a Gene Autry Melody Rancher guitar that Gibson Guitar Company put out in the '40s. It belonged to Joe Gunter from Big Spring Valley. He was my wife Shirley's cousin. His wife Kathleen gave it to me after he died. Joe and Kathleen always supported my music.

The Melody Rancher was a famous guitar along Highway 79 South in Blount County because it was one of the first guitars that Berl Barnes (an original member of one of the first bluegrass bands in our area, the Warrior River Boys) played when he walked from his house to Brooksville, where his mother was postmaster. Berl was always one of my musical heroes, going back to the heyday of radio on Sand Mountain, Alabama.

Lonnie William "Wild Bill" Prickett Sr. was a colorful radio announcer and songwriter who loved cowboy music, country music, string band music and bluegrass music. I went to a lot of fiddlers' conventions at which he was the master of ceremonies, and I ended up being a judge at a lot of them. It was a lot of fun, and I learned a lot about old-time string band and bluegrass music. Raymond Fairchild, from Maggie Valley, North Carolina, was a successful competing banjo player in those days before he became famous.

Tom Prickett and Richard Burgess, who were the comedy team of Arley and Charley, were the authors of songs like "Old Sand Mountain Home" and "Johnny Get Your Gun." These two songs, as well as several others, were recorded by the Warrior River Boys.

Ethridge Scott played the banjo so well that Earl Scruggs heard him and thought it was his own playing. Berl ended up playing the Dobro guitar. D.M. Fox played the mandolin and Gary Thurman played the guitar. There are several others who played with the band over the years, and even today the Warrior River Boys still are making music in some form or fashion. Bill, Gary and others have passed on.

Berl moved to California after his wife, Sue, died and played in a band out there before he died. He always came to see us when he visited home from California. Tom and his wife Lois got to where they couldn't go anywhere and went to be with their daughter in Columbus, Georgia.

As a side note, I met my friend Gary Thurman in Boaz when he was running a cowboy movie theatre that only showed Gene Autry movies and other old westerns. We became good friends. He worked for a man who had a complete collection of Gene Autry movies and a lot of memorabilia. Gary also passed on after a notable career in bluegrass and other ventures. It is my understanding that he helped Gene restore and replace a lot of his things from the Alabama collection when Gene's museum burned down and a lot of his things were destroyed.

I always thought that cowboy music was the best. I started studying it at an early age. I read Jack Thorpe, the Lomax books, Botkin and other nonfiction cowboy songbooks. I listened to as many of the Library of Congress tapes and records as possible. Like most historical or real old-time music, only the words were recorded in the form of poetry until the researchers went out in the field and started collecting by recording and writing down the notes as they heard them. Many tunes were lost but the words were saved.

My dream to be a cowboy continued only in my music. I never bought a horse, although I have ridden many. I guess I was always lucky with horses because I never had a bad incident. I have bought some fancy hats, boots and shirts and learned how to do some cowboy yodeling, as well as some great cowboy songs.

A few years ago at the DuQuoin State Fair in Illinois, I stumbled across a chuck wagon show complete with storytelling and campfire. The only music they had was courtesy of a wonderful harmonica player named Bud, a half Mexican/half Jewish bass player named Doc Lopez and Bud's son, Rusty Rankin. I fell in love with their act and all that went with it.

I joined them for two years, and we traveled Texas, Louisiana, Alabama, Illinois, Maryland, Tennessee, Nevada and Pennsylvania together. I finally got my chance to feel like a real cowboy. Sitting around the campfire with Bud's harmonica, my guitar and Rusty playing on the gutbucket bass was as real as it could get for me. I really enjoyed it.

I will always have the memory of the good times Rusty, Bud and I shared with "Rusty's Trail Blazing Chuckwagon and Western Show": the songs, the stories, the food and the camaraderie. Partners on the trail. Thank you Bud and Rusty for what I learned from you and for helping me accomplish my '50s dream.

Just like all us little boys back in Huntsville, I sat in the movie theatre watching my heroes ride across the screen. I've been to a lot of rodeos, western shows, roundups and other cowboy stuff. Always liked it, always will—'cause I always wanted to be a cowboy.

MY FIRST STEAK

"Living it up in a first-class restaurant."

Huntsville, Alabama, was a bustling town in the '50s. People were moving in right and left and construction was booming. Schools weren't big enough (some schoolrooms had as many as fifty children in them). People were living in motels waiting for houses to be built or rented.

I remember doing a lot of things for the first time growing up in Huntsville: roller-skating on the Madison County Courthouse Square on Christmas when everyone got their first pair of clamp-on roller skates; going to the movies without an adult; hitchhiking around town; motor scooters (the Cushman Eagle was the most popular, and I wanted one); and the 165 Harley-Davidson motorcycle (Gary Lawson had one, and so did Tommy Huskey). Gary liked motorcycles. He ended up with a motorcycle shop in town and later went into the real estate business.

I remember everyone smoking or wanting to smoke. We were even allowed to smoke on the back porch at Butler High School (called Butler High but had grades six through twelve when I first went there).

I remember Boogertown and all the other places like it. Boogertown was "company housing" that eventually became run-down and was later called a slum. I had a lot of friends that lived there with whom I grew up when I went to Butler High School.

One of my fondest and most memorable moments was the opportunity to eat in a restaurant and order anything I wanted to eat. I was in the DeMolay

West Clinton classroom, 1950.

(a Masonic organization for young men age fourteen to twenty-one), and we were asked to help the Lions Club sell light bulbs door-to-door. The proceeds, of course, would go to the Lions Club for aid and assistance to the blind and people with sight problems. We were assigned an adult to supervise our sales. We loaded up car trunks with cases of light bulbs. The adult would let us out at the end of a street, and we would go door-to-door with the light bulbs. Most people paid in cash. I had never seen that much money in all my fourteen years.

We sold a lot of light bulbs. When we finished, we all met back at the place where we started. Each one of the adults took his team out to eat. The light bulb sales leader took us to James Steakhouse. I had never been in James Steakhouse on the courthouse square. The owner was the father of a girl I knew from church and school. Of course his name was James, and her name was Marie. They were Greeks.

The idea of going out to eat when I was growing up was not a common one in our house. We only went out to eat when we went on a long trip.

James was Greek so you could smell the seasonings when you walked in the door. I liked the smell then and I still like the smell now. They told us we could have anything we wanted to eat. I lagged back to see what everyone else was ordering. The man asked us if we liked steak.

We all said yes.

Glimpses of Huntsville in the 1950s

Kids in Boogertown in the 1950s.

Up until that time, I had never eaten a steak in a restaurant. People didn't eat steaks like they do today. Barbecue grills were not common yet, and no one knew much about cooking on charcoal. Most steaks (if you had them) were cooked in a cast-iron skillet on top of the stove. We all ordered steak.

They asked us how we wanted it cooked. I ordered mine medium like most of the others. We all got a salad, baked potato and New York strip steak. It looked like it weighed a pound. It was brought out on a sizzling platter. I enjoyed every morsel of it while living it up in a first-class restaurant. I still think of that first steak when I am eating one today and remember how much I appreciated it then and how much I appreciate it now.

As a side note, Marie and I remained friends throughout our childhood until her death a few years ago. We had many laughs and reminiscences about the first steak I ever ate in a fancy restaurant, as well as other times we shared growing up in Huntsville in the '50s.

MY OLD TRUCK CAN SWIM

"It ain't how deep it is, it's how shallow it is."
—Mark Twain

Back in the good old days, when the automobile was mostly American and cars seemed to last forever, I obtained a 1953 GMC pickup truck. I bought it from a used car dealer on Meridian Street. It was sitting in a row of cars on the back lot called fishing cars.

These were the older models or rougher-looking models that were still running and might get you where you were going. You had to be careful to check everything when you bought one of these cars because they may have been rigged up just to sell. Sawdust in the transmission, heavy-duty motor oil so it would not leak so fast, tape on hoses and more.

I liked the truck. It had a six-cylinder engine and four-on-the-floor transmission. The speedometer only went to eighty. It had a rebel flag tag on the front and it was painted light green. Pretty good paint job. Some of the paint was still on the windows and tires. All of the tires were good and the windshield wipers worked. Hand painted on the side were the words "The Rebel." I couldn't wait to show it to my buddy Jimmy Ellis.

He was one of my fishing buddies, and his boat would fit in the back of the pickup truck. He liked my truck and we planned our first fishing trip. We were going to the Elk River to spend a couple of nights with his boat and my new (old) truck. Saturday morning came and we lit out.

Washington Street from North Square.

It started raining not too long after we left the house. We stopped and got some ice to put in the cooler and pick up a few things. When we turned off the highway Jimmy asked me how much play there was in the steering because I almost knocked down several mailboxes. I told him that it had a little play and that I could handle it. I did notice that the steering was getting worse.

We pulled off the main road on to a dirt road that would take us over to the spot on the river we desired. It sure was muddy and slippery and sort of washed out, but we proceeded on. As we started up a small winding hill road, we started slipping. I couldn't control the truck. It started sliding down the bank and we landed in the water. In the Elk River.

The truck stayed afloat as we drifted across a slough and got stuck on the bottom. Now I am sure that most people would be cussing or crying or yelling or squirming around as mad as a wet hen. We just sat there in our seats as cool as a cucumber.

Jimmy lit up a cigarette, put the pack back up in the visor where it would not get wet and proceeded to pull off his cowboy boots. He was from El Paso, Texas, and was one of the few people I knew growing up who wore cowboy boots. I watched him pour the water out of them and place them on top of the truck. Then he got out, waded back to the bank and took off walking. I asked him where he was going, and he said he was going to get some help. He told me to stay put and that he would be back directly. I sat there in the cab full of water like a dummy for a pretty good while. Then I heard the sound of a motor.

It was a tractor. Jimmy had gone to a farmer and told him of our plight. He hooked the tractor up to the truck and gently pulled us out of the water. When we got on the bank and unhooked, Jimmy thanked the farmer and the tractor went put-putting off.

Jimmy raised the hood, wiped a few things off and told me to hit the switch. I pushed the starter button and it cranked right up. Jimmy had a big old Texas-know-it-all, I-know-what-I'm-doing kind of smile on his face, and then the sun came out.

We drove for a long time to find the right place to put in, but we still went fishing that day. By golly my old GMC could swim. It had swum plum across the Elk River.

My buddy from El Paso and I made a lot of trips to the river in that old truck. The play in the steering wheel kept getting worse, the pretty green paint job started wearing off and that old speedometer never got to eighty miles per hour.

Jimmy remained my fishing buddy for a long time until one day when he disappeared. Years later I discovered that he had been in Thailand for quite some time. He came to visit me several times, and we went fishing. We remained friends until he passed away. We always laughed about the two fools who slid off the road into Elk River and watched their truck swim across the river and drive away.

SHARECROPPIN'

"My friend Jim"

Growing up in the '40s and '50s was a good experience in Madison County, Alabama. The end of World War II and the returning soldiers changed our country.

With the exception of the Korean Conflict (it was a "war" for those who went to Korea or had friends or relatives who did) and the Cold War, our country was at peace with the world. States that had been struggling to get out of the Great Depression were slowly getting ahead.

One of the biggest changes in the South was in Madison County, Alabama, the introduction and growth of rockets and missiles at Redstone Arsenal. It seemed like change, modernization and the space age happened overnight. Huntsville would never be the same little sleepy town with a courthouse and Big Spring.

There were still a lot of things that hadn't changed yet and one of them was the sharecropper. The sharecropper was a farmer who tilled and worked the soil and harvested the crop to be brought to market. After it was sold, the costs were subtracted, and the owner gave the sharecropper his share of what had been agreed on.

The sharecropper usually did not own anything except a few personal belongings. He usually did his shopping on credit at a particular store or two, and his bill was paid when the crop came in.

My friend Jim was the son of a sharecropper. Jim was my best friend even though we came from two different backgrounds. He lived in a two-

Cotton hand picking.

room home (could be described by many today as a tar paper shack with brown imitation brick–pattern tar paper). But to us it was his home and we were buddies.

Jim's sister, younger brother and his mom and dad were nice to me. I used to spend the night with them in the summers. We would sleep outside on the porch or over by the mule shed or chicken house. His mom and dad slept in one room on one side of the house, and they had a blanket hung from the rafter to divide the room because his grandmother slept in the other half of the room. Jim and his sister and brother slept in the part that had the kitchen, with linoleum floors and a big old wood cookstove.

The only electric connection hung down in the kitchen over the table, and it had a plug-in for the radio when they played it. They had an outhouse out back and chamber pots in the house for toilet needs.

When I would visit or spend the night, Jim's mother always made big pots of stew, soup, chili or dumplings. I didn't realize for years that we ate those big pots of soupy stew because there wasn't enough meat to go around like we have today.

Jim was smart in school and was a good influence on me. We both liked to read and tell each other about what we had read. He liked science and math and such. I liked literature, adventure, geography, history and traveling. Together we made an interesting pair because we told stories to each other about what we were studying or reading. We learned from each other by being friends.

We'd go on adventure trips to the river and make little rafts and boats, catch lots of catfish and trap a rabbit or two. At night in late August, when it was scorching hot in the day and cool at night, we'd lie in the cracked red clay between the rows of cotton that was still green. We'd look up at the stars at night and watch for shooting stars, comets and other things like a slow-moving plane. We'd wonder where it was going or where it was coming from. Jim could name all the planets that were visible and the different craters on the moon, as well as other sights in the sky. He knew all about weather, clouds and lightning and thunder.

His dream was to explore space. He wanted to ride off into space in a rocket. Of course, today we call them guided missiles and the people who go to space are called astronauts. That was his dream. My dream was to see the world, make music and be a travelin' man. I rambled on about pirates and sled dogs and mountain climbing. Together we taught each other everything we could glean from books, school and other sources. We went all through our school years helping each other with our lessons and running around together. Lots of good times were spent together, and then we graduated from high school and left home. We said our goodbyes, promising to stay in touch and keep up with each other.

I guess when you leave home for the excitement of the world, you sometimes lose track of staying in touch with friends from back home. Jim came to my mind quite often, but I was not much of a letter writer so I lost touch with him. Then one day I went back home and decided that I would try to find out Jim's location.

I went out to where the field of cotton was and discovered that it was very much changed. It had been replaced with a housing subdivision. There were streets, curbs, a strip mall, a post office and lots of other buildings. Nothing was the same except for an old grocery store out on the old highway that was still in business.

I went in and was immediately recognized by Jim's younger brother, who was now operating the store. We were glad to see each other. We got us a Double Cola and went out on the porch to catch up.

His dad and mom moved into town to the old mill village, and his sister had gotten married to a soldier from California who was stationed at Redstone Arsenal. Jim's brother had married his high school sweetheart and lived in a house down the old highway.

Clinton Street, Dunnavants Department Store on right.

Well, what about Jim! Jim had gone into the U.S. Air Force. He had made such high scores on the tests that they sent him to Massachusetts Institute of Technology (MIT). He graduated from there with honors, and they made him an officer. He was sent to Houston, Texas, after learning how to fly jets and other aircraft. He ended up training the astronauts who got to go into space.

Even though he could not go himself, he accomplished his dream through those men and women we sent into space over the years. Eventually, I met up with Jim just after he retired from the air force as a colonel. He married a girl from New York State who taught him how to speak correctly, dance and which fork to use at the table.

He now had the manners of a gentleman and the appearance of success. He and his wife bought a big house out in the country in Tennessee, and he has horses in front of his house out on a huge white-fenced pasture. Down at the bottom of the hill in a grove of trees next to the creek is a little dog-run cabin he has built. It's not like the one in which he grew up, but he says that it reminds him of home.

When I visit him, we go down to the cabin, sit out on the porch and talk for hours about the old days of adventure and books, where we have been and about the cabin in the cotton. On a clear night, when the stars are out, we lie down on our backs and look up at the sky in wonderment and spin tales of yesteryear. We talk about our dreams and the past. Jim and I talk about the good old days and sharecroppin' in the cotton.

I remembered the last time that I was in a field of cotton. It was with my friend Wayne Short. He had an Allstate motor scooter. It was one of those days when we had nothing to do but ride around on his scooter looking for something to do. A friend had told us that you could get four dollars per one hundred pounds cotton out on the west end of Madison County. We headed out that way bright and early the next morning and picked cotton all day. We made about four dollars apiece and thought it was big money. Most of the people picking that day were black. It was hard work. Backbreaking! I don't think I would have made a good sharecropper.

Cotton picking machinery changed everything.

Wayne ended up working in the mines in Jefferson County, Alabama, until he retired. Wayne and I weren't very good cotton pickers, but my friend Jim was.

RIVER PIRATES ON THE TENNESSEE

"I never ran away—I always ran to."

The river always drew me. I was mystified by it—continuously flowing by and ending up who knows where.

During the '50s, a lot of fishermen and people who had business on the river kept a wooden skiff or flat-bottomed boat chained to a tree or hidden in the bushes. Some of them were in pretty good shape and were painted up with green or gray paint. Some of them were forgotten and left unattended too long and were not in such good shape.

Ricky Bogel and Jimmy Ellis and I stumbled on one such old dilapidated boat one afternoon while we were camping down on the river out near the old Whitesburg Bridge. We had seen it many times before, and it had been a long time since anyone had used it.

We decided that it was abandoned and that we would commandeer it for our use. We managed to tear the chain off the old willow tree to which it was attached and clean it up. It was floatable and we put it in the water.

With a couple of makeshift poles and a homemade paddle, we set out to cross the river. Soon after we took off and crossed the river, we decided to drift with the river for a while. We had not thought about how we were going to get back across the river.

Pretty soon we were moving along pretty fast and out of control. There was an old Sir Walter Riley Tobacco can that we had carried along to use

Ms. Guntersville, Mobile tug.

for a bailing bucket. We needed to get back across the river on the Huntsville side but couldn't manage to get over.

We ended up in the middle of the river and out of control. We weren't lost, but we felt like we were because we had no control over where we were going. We began to pass Redstone Arsenal and then Triana—too far for our yells to be heard. When we did get someone's attention, all they did was wave back.

It was beginning to get dark, and the mosquitoes were coming out in droves, as well as the evening deerflies. Man those flies sure could hurt. Ricky, who was light-complexioned, was the most vulnerable. Jimmy, who always acted tough and never complained, just kept that old Texas smile on his face.

I guess I had a worried look on my face, because I knew we were in trouble in more ways than one. None of us had a watch, and in those days no one had a cellphone to call for help. We were in the current and there was no getting out of it.

We could see lights on the banks in the distance, it was pitch-black out and there was no moon. Maybe a trotliner would come by on the way to run his lines and he could help us out. It's dangerous to be on the river at night without a flashlight or some kind of illumination.

In the distance I could see and hear the sounds of a barge line coming. Its lights were focused on what was in front of it. We knew that we were not in its path, but we were afraid of the big wake it would make. We yelled our lungs out as it came by, but nobody was looking our way and it passed.

It threw a four-foot wake right at us and swamped our boat. We all managed to all hold on for dear life. Now we were in a real pickle. The boat was upside down but still afloat as we all crawled up on top of it to figure out our next move. We didn't want to leave one another and try to swim to the bank. We knew that we would eventually come to Decatur and that there would be a lot of activity there.

As we drifted along, we began to get more comfortable with our situation even though we were wet, tired and hungry. No one would be looking for us because everyone knew we were supposed to be out on the river camping, as we had often done.

The lights of Decatur started to glow on the horizon as we drifted that way. The current carried us over to the Decatur side, and the first place we came to was the feed mills. They had lights and equipment going everywhere.

We managed to grab on to a barge hold and climb up to the top. Of course it was an off-limits area, and soon the guard saw us coming up the hill.

"Where in the world did you boys come from?" he asked.

It must have been a shocker for him to see the three soppy-looking river pirates. We told him part of what happened, and he led us to the front gate.

After a long walk out to the highway back to Huntsville, we were headed home. We hitched a ride in the back of a pickup truck and then back out to the river fourteen miles from town.

Daylight came just as we got back to our campsite. We built a fire, cooked some bacon and all took a well-earned snooze.

We had many adventures on the river and lots of stories to tell about it. I miss those days of our youth when we were free to come and go and do things like camp on the river, fish, hunt and trap. Jimmy Ellis and Ricky Bogel have both died, but they left me with some good memories of growing up in Huntsville in the '50s.

THOU SHALT NOT STEAL
A PAIR OF RED SOCKS

"Peer pressure was with us in the '50s too."

Kids in Huntsville used to walk great distances to either go to school, visit someone or go to town. On any given weekday after school was out or on Saturday mornings, you could find a bunch of kids downtown. Most of the time, they didn't cause anyone trouble, and the store clerks and operators welcomed their visits to dream and look around.

If you weren't in the movie theatre, you were probably walking around with friends, in the basement of Montgomery Wards on the Square, hanging out at Tom Dark's City Drugstore, playing basketball at the YMCA, looking around the five and dime store or going in and out of all the stores downtown.

I was downtown one afternoon with a couple of friends carousing around, and one of the boys started a dare. He dared everyone to each go in a store and steal something. I was afraid at the thought. I knew that it was wrong right from the start. My dad and mom instilled in me and my two brothers the belief that stealing was wrong. If you did steal something, you would be punished. George Ferrell, my Sunday school teacher, taught us right from wrong.

One of the boys went into Tom Dark's City Drugstore on the east side of the square and stole a magazine. It was the *New Yorker*, an expensive magazine. Another went into the hardware store and stole a small padlock and key. One of the other boys went into the basement at Montgomery Wards, got a whole bag of popcorn and slipped out without paying. I was

South side square, Harrison Brothers.

the oldest and biggest in the group, and the pressure was on me to really do something big. Dunnavants Department Store was chosen for my target.

It was a nice store with a main floor, basement and upper level, on which the men's department was. We went up there first, and the manager of that department gave us a dirty look. We all left and went outside. I thought that I was going to get out of doing anything, but the pressure was still on. I went back in the side entrance by myself and went down to the bargain basement. Without looking around or acting like anything was wrong, I walked over to a counter and grabbed a pair of red wool socks. I stuffed them in my pocket and proceeded up the stairs and toward the front door where my friends would be waiting across the street.

When I got to the door, there was a very tall, large man that looked a little like Santa Claus. He had one hand on his hip and the other against the side of the doorway. I stopped dead in my tracks. I had been caught. He was the manager of the bargain basement and had obviously seen me commit the dastardly deed. He asked me if I knew what I had done. He said that I had two choices to make. One was to pay for the socks and walk away. The other was to return the socks to the counter in the bargain basement. I returned

Clinton Street business scene.

them to the basement. I thought for a moment that this was all there was going to be to it, but it wasn't. I thought about my mom and dad and what they were going to do. What would be my punishment? I thought about Mr. George Ferrell, my Sunday school teacher and friend of our family. I thought about Mr. Faber, my scoutmaster.

Then Mr. Smith, the basement department manager, approached me again and stared right down into my face: "John, why did you do this? You have let me and everyone else down by stealing. Stealing is wrong and you know it. What are you going to do about it?" I guess I looked like the cat that ate the canary because I was as guilty as sin and knew it. I knew right from wrong, I told him. I asked him what I could do to make things right. Anything! He told me that he would let me go and not say anything to anyone about this if I would promise not to ever do it again. I promised and I meant it. He patted me on the shoulder and told me to get gone. Whew, what a sigh of relief it was to walk out the front door of Dunnavants Department Store in Huntsville a free man again.

Standing right across the street were my buddies. They were laughing their heads off. I didn't know what to say to them. I was so glad to be out

Huntsville High School building front.

of the situation I had gotten myself into that I didn't care what they said. I told them what happened. They hung on to every word. As we were walking along the sidewalk back beside Dunnavants, out popped Mr. Smith. He asked Milton where he got the *New Yorker* magazine that was rolled up in his back pocket. He asked George were he had gotten the padlock and key that was attached to his belt loop. He asked Lee where he had gotten the bag of popcorn. We had all been caught! Mr. Smith gave us another lecture about the difference between right and wrong. Then he let us go.

To this day I have not forgotten this. When I graduated from Huntsville High School, I got a shirt and tie from him, as well as a tie clasp that I still use until this day. It is a replica of a Model 870 Remington shotgun. It is slightly tarnished, but I have worn it all these years and can't help but think about Mr. Smith and the lesson I learned from him. Milton and George went in the U.S. Marine Corps. Lee moved to California and ended up in prison for murder. I am lucky that I listened to Mr. Smith. The '50s were full of Mr. Smiths. They were called role models—men of character. Huntsville had its share of them. Thou shalt not steal a pair of red socks.

ZESTO BURGERS, DIP DOGS, HAMBURGERS AND CHILI DOGS

"Some good old eatin' places in Huntsville"

Not everyone cares to remember the first hamburger they had, but I remember the first good hamburger I ever had. It was at the Big Spring Café down next to the Big Spring Canal in downtown Huntsville. I remember that it had mustard, onions and two slices of dill pickle with salt and pepper. That's what most of the hamburger places put on a hamburger. The hamburgers were full of fillers, crackers, bread, meal and more.

Wimpy's Grill on the east side of the courthouse square was another classic hamburger of the day. It cooked a whole pan full and let them sit in hot water until they were ordered. They sure were juicy! There was a blinking neon sign out in front of the restaurant with the character Wimpy from the cartoon *Popeye*.

Then there was the Snow White on the square. Red Bennett, his wife and son ran that place. They were our next-door neighbors when we lived on Brook Manor Street. Best chili in town! They had twelve hamburgers for one dollar—little square burgers on little square buns with mustard, onions and pickle. Later, a freestanding Snow White was built in place a few blocks from the hospital and they added barbecue. It became a popular hangout for Huntsville High students.

Zesto.

Another hangout for high school students was Jerry's Drive-in on the Memorial Parkway. Of course, since it was a drive-in, you had to be in a car to get waited on. There were a lot of things that went on at Jerry's. Huntsville, Butler and the new Lee High Schools all congregated there in the evenings. You never knew what was going to happen among the students from the three schools. A lot of folks with cars would cruise as many drive-ins as they could on Friday or Saturday nights. Since Huntsville was growing so fast because of the space program, there were new places to go every year.

The Zesto at Five Points was a most unusual but familiar place. You walked up to the service window and ordered what you wanted. It was famous for two things: the Zesto Burger and the Dip Dog. It also had good soft-serve ice cream. The Zesto Burger was a hamburger with seasonings and filler, very much like a meatball, which was breaded, put on a stick and deep fat fried. The Dip Dog was a deep fat fried wiener on a stick with cornmeal breading. A lot of people call them corn dogs. Houston Goodson owned the Zesto. He was very active with the youth and was a DeMolay advisor at the Twickenham Chapter of the Order of DeMolay, which met in the Helion Masonic Lodge. I became a member of that DeMolay chapter when I was fourteen years old. The Masonic Lodge building is one of the oldest buildings in the state.

There were lots of places that served hot dogs with chili, but the top two places for me were Mullin's in Old Huntsville and Phillip's Lunchroom on Seminole Drive. Of course they were called chili dogs.

Glimpses of Huntsville in the 1950s

Steadman's Restaurant on West Holmes and the Southland on Governor's Drive were two old standby places to eat. I believe I remember the Hastings family running the Southland. Their son's name was Don and I knew him at Butler School. Danny Banks lived across the road from the Southland. He was in the band at Butler and played the trumpet. He was also the drum major in the band. He later became a lawyer and a judge in Huntsville. He also played in a band that was and still is popular with high school reunions. It was very much like the Beach Boys.

Henry's Hamburger Drive-in was located across from Rison School on Oakwood.

The Fox Restaurant located on what is now Governor's Drive is another place long forgotten. The Fox family ran it all during the '50s, and their son graduated from Huntsville High in 1958. They had a sign out front with a red fox on it that stated that the restaurant was air-conditioned. It later became Red Bennett's restaurant. Bingo! We had two Red Bennetts that owned restaurants in Huntsville. A lot of people would walk from the Huntsville Hospital to eat there.

Shoney's built a place on the Parkway. You could use the drive-in or you could eat in the restaurant. It had the best milkshakes in town, topped with real whipped cream and a cherry. Shoney's had a hamburger called the Big Boy. It was the first double-decker hamburger I ever ate. It had a three-piece specially made bun with a particular sauce that was kind of like Thousand Island salad dressing. I still love it to this day.

Although there was plenty of north Alabama pit barbecue to be had in the Huntsville area, Gibson's Barbeque Restaurant was the most popular. Gibson's started in Decatur by Big Bob Gibson, and the Huntsville Gibson's was owned by the Hampton family. I went to Huntsville High School with John Paul Hampton. His mother was a Gibson. They had good sauce and knew how to hickory smoke pork shoulders on an open pit. Gibson's also had some of the best barbecued chicken around. They used small chickens, and they were always cooked good and tender. Gibson's had an "all you can eat" special on the fried chicken. I won't give his last name, but someone named Richard was asked not to come back for the "all you can eat" special. Yes, the chickens were small, but more than four or five was too many for one man to eat without putting Gibson's out of business.

If you really wanted a treat you could drive out to the old Greenbriar Restaurant in Greenbriar. They had the best barbecue and catfish. The barbecue was cooked the old way: over a hickory smoked fire, good and slow, with patience and real hickory. The catfish were brought in fresh daily in big washtubs from the Tennessee River. The tables at the old Greenbriar were made out of plywood, and some of them were still in use the last time I was there.

Barbecue cooked over an open pit with hickory wood was what we typically called north Alabama barbecue. It was simple. An old black man told me long ago that you should not mess with the meat on a pit if it was going to be done right. He said not to poke it, stick it or grab it—good, sweet, pink, slow-cooked and tender pork. Shoulders were the best, but any part of a pig would do. Texas has its beef cooked on mesquite wood, but we have our pork over hickory wood.

There was always a discussion about who had the best sauce or what kind of sauce was the best: sweet sauce, hot sauce, tomato-based sauce, mustard sauce, white sauce and just plain old barbecue sauce. We had them all. Most barbecue in restaurants today is cooked with gas or cooked in foil in an oven. The barbecue cooked in the contests that are held today would not have been affordable back in the '50s, due to all of the fancy ingredients in their sauces, rubs and marinades. The cookers they use today would not have been affordable by the common man. A few concrete blocks and a grill or a fifty-five-gallon drum was all that was needed. Huntsville and surrounding communities had many barbecue places that sold nothing but the cooked meat. Nearby New Hope, Monrovia, New Market, Gurley and Hazel Green all had good barbecue.

Nothing could beat the blue-plate specials at the Bon Air Restaurant on Meridian Street. It was built in 1951 by the Hicks family and remained in the family until its demise as a result of the construction of Interstate 565. The restaurant had the best beef stew anywhere I have ever been and some of the best cornbread sticks to go with the stew. Many bragged about the yeast rolls and fresh vegetables.

A hamburger steak at the Rebel Inn across from the old Butler High School was also fantastic.

The Try Me Drive In Restaurant on Triana was another good place to eat dinner. They had homemade yeast rolls. They lost a lot of business because someone was supposed to have been killed in the restaurant. I wasn't there, so I am not going to say who got killed or how they got killed.

One thing we had back then that has disappeared from sight is the "tamale man." Huntsville Park is where he headquartered, and he sold the best tamales in the world. My mom and dad loved them, and we used to cook a pot of chili and go get a couple of dozen with a box of fresh crackers. It was a real treat.

Glimpses of Huntsville in the 1950s

We never really had any Mexican places until the El Palacio came to town in the 1960s. A man drove in from Texas and brought a bunch of his family and friends and started it. Later on, he sold franchises and did pretty well. They were located all over the South, and the one in Huntsville is still going strong and is just as popular as ever.

We didn't have any Chinese places that I remember in the '50s. It seemed like they were everywhere at one time. The Golden Dragon on Jordan Lane was always my favorite. Later, the Formosa on University was also great because of their crab legs and succulent barbecue ribs.

To me, the two fanciest restaurants we had in Huntsville were the Dwarf off Governor's Drive and the Parkway and the Ritz in downtown Huntsville. I had my first lobster at the Dwarf, and the Ritz always had something different to eat.

Some of the old places are still around, like Mullins and Big Spring No. 2, and there are a lot of new and different businesses. I will always remember the savory taste of that first good hamburger and the good old days in Huntsville.

Miss Edna Keel, one of my teachers at Huntsville High School, once made the announcement that Huntsville was going to get an Albert Pick Motel. She said that Huntsville had really arrived and that we would be on the map some day. Boy was she right! The Albert Pick has since long been gone and Huntsville sure has arrived.

THE CORNET, THE BANJO
AND THE BUFFALO

"Two cultures in the same place"

The segregation of the races existed in Huntsville in the '50s just as it did in most of the United States and particularly in the South. We were not taught to think segregation. It was just a way of life, and for most of us young white people we never gave it much thought.

I don't ever remember mistreating or disrespecting anyone, but I may have and been unaware. I was always interested in boxing, so I had dealings with black people who were involved in the sport. I also knew Uncle Mose when I was younger and learned a lot from him. He had told me about the great fighters of the past. He never discussed race with me or led me to believe that he had any problems with segregation. I did know that he had to go all the way across town to go to the bathroom or get something to eat or drink. I didn't realize that it was because he was black.

Oscar Burns, an elderly black gentleman and the janitor at the Episcopal Church of the Nativity, was a friend to all of us young boys. I remember getting a cornet horn for Christmas and wanting to learn how to play it. I was thirteen years old and loved to hear Dixieland jazz and big-band music. I took it down to the furnace room at the church, in which Oscar had his own little place all fixed up. He had a coffeepot on a burner and some pots and things to cook soup. He had a bed and little bathroom just for him.

He lit up when he saw my horn. I could tell he wanted to play it but was afraid to ask. I told him to go ahead. I washed the mouthpiece off in his sink and dried it off for him. You would have thought that I was listening to Louis Armstrong. When he finished, he showed me a few fundamental things that worked for me. He washed the mouthpiece off and handed it back to me. Oscar could play the horn.

He asked me if I had ever heard of W.C. Handy. I told him no. He told me all about Mr. Handy, how he was from Alabama and had taught music in Huntsville. He wrote "St. Louis Blues" and lots of other pieces and is known as the "Father of the Blues." He said that a lot of black people were musicians today because of him. I assumed that this was where Oscar learned how to play. Little did I know how proud I would be to have had that moment with Oscar.

I eventually became a professional musician and entertainer. Oscar was one of my encouragers. Even though Oscar was black, I never thought about him as black. He was just a nice, jolly older man who always had a kind word and wanted to help.

Years later, I was sitting on a bale of hay at the San Antonio Rodeo and Livestock Show in San Antonio, Texas. I was there for seventeen days as an entertainer, singing cowboy songs and playing my guitar and banjo. I had my own one-man stage and it was at ground level. A lot of people stopped to talk to me or to catch my show. I liked the audiences and all of the people who stopped.

Every morning a black man walked by in a U.S. Army Buffalo Soldier uniform. He was one of the living history reenactors portraying the black Buffalo Soldier of yesteryear. He always waved at me but was always in a hurry and never stopped by until one morning when I motioned for him to come over and sit down.

I wanted to hear all about the Buffalo Soldiers. He explained to me that they were a black group of cavalry and that he was just getting started with the reenactors. I learned that he had just retired from the army and was taking up a new hobby as a Buffalo Soldier. He said that he had a lot to learn.

I told him that he looked good in his uniform. It was brand new, and his boots were shined as good as they could be. He said that his father had been a professional soldier. I told him that mine had, too. He said he was from the South. I told him I was too. I asked him where. He told me he was from Huntsville. I told him I was too. I asked him where he lived and where he went to school. He said he graduated from Council High in 1960. I told him I graduated from Huntsville High in 1960. We compared notes.

He had been in the Boy Scouts just as I had been. His Scout troop was black. We compared notes on growing up in the '50s and what it was like for

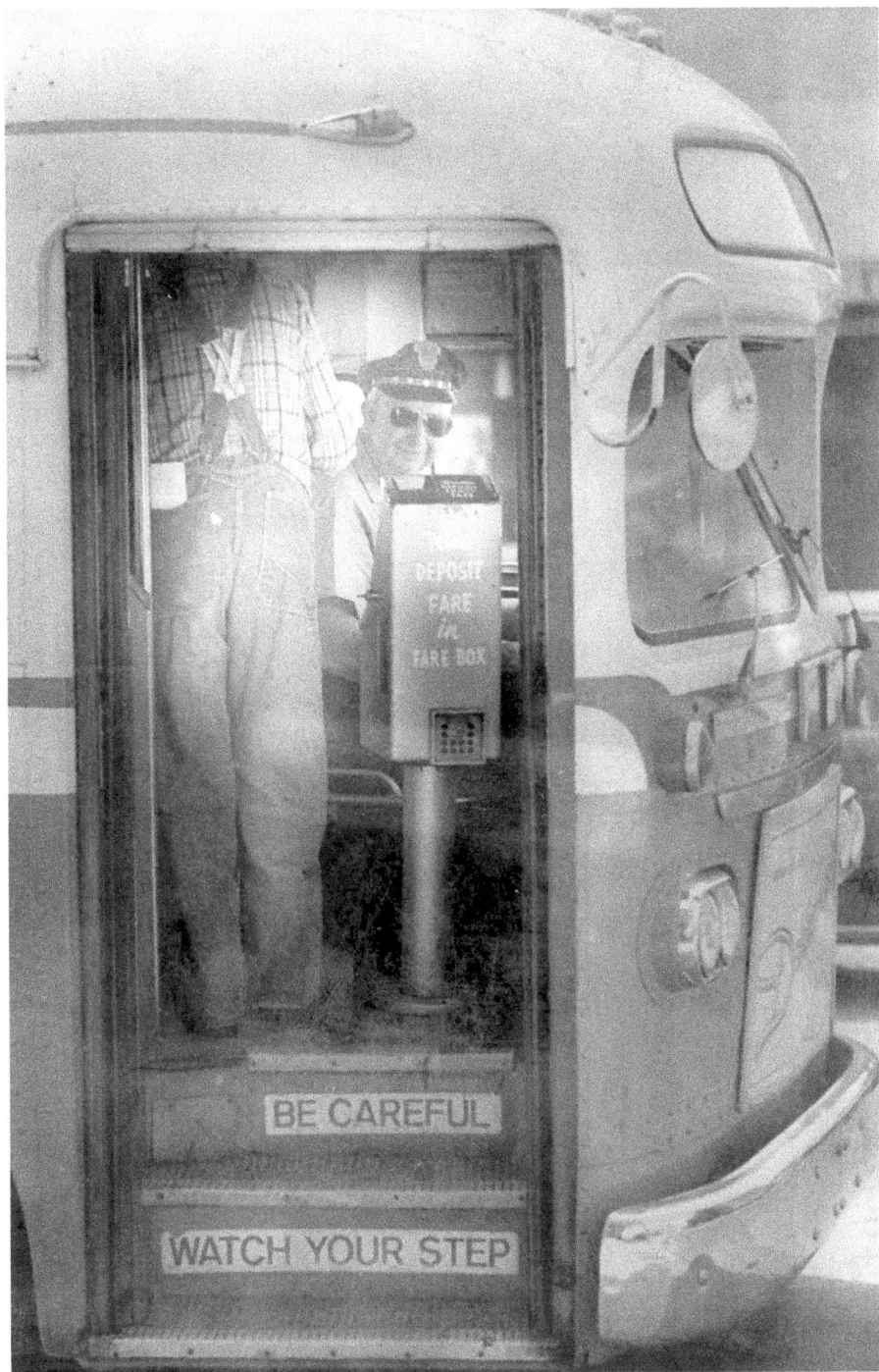

Bus driver James Carter.

each other. We talked about segregation and how things have changed. He said that he had been back to Huntsville but that it was so different he didn't care for it anymore. He liked the old Huntsville of the '50s better.

He said that he had enjoyed growing up in Huntsville. He enjoyed his school, church and friends and that the people in town had always been nice to him. We knew some of the same people and had been in some of the same places at the same time.

How fascinating it was to hear about segregated Huntsville from the viewpoint of a man who grew up as neighbor I didn't know in the '50s—two different cultures under the same umbrella.

A happenstance meeting connected to a cornet, banjo and buffalo. Two cultures in the same place.

WHISKEY, BOOTLEGGING
AND PURPLE PASSION

"As seen through the eyes of an observer, ahem."

This is a subject that can get you in trouble if you start remembering too much from the past about anything to do with alcohol. I must say that from my own observations that too much of it is not healthy for you or anybody whom you are around. I am not condoning it or honoring it, nor am I promoting the sale of it. I can remember some of the things that alcohol had to do with my life that were not good.

Back in the '50s around Huntsville, there were people from whom you could buy whiskey and beer, which were illegal. We called them bootleggers. Some of them would sell alcohol to minors. I'm not going to tell on them now, even though most of them are dead. I am going to say that as a young boy I could go to a house within sight of Huntsville Hospital and purchase whiskey. They would sell it by the drink to go, the scant, quart, gallon or case. If you bought it by the drink, you usually got a coke with the top poured off and the rest in whiskey with wax paper and a rubber band around it. That could cost as much as a dollar in the late '50s.

Other places had a spot to sit down and have a drink or a place where you could get served in your car. The most ingenious was set up like a picnic area with lights strung in the trees, a jukebox and picnic tables. They even had ice cream and cold soda drinks for the family, as well as sandwiches and snacks. One of these two places was just over the mountain on Monte Sano. The farthest one away for a Sunday afternoon drive was a place called Little

Whitesburg Drive, aerial.

New York, which was near Guntersville State Park. It had a pet monkey and other attractions for the family. It's amazing how it made drinking a family activity. These places were always busy and never seemed to get in trouble with the law.

Drinking and smoking was something that a lot of people were doing in those days. Of course the Veterans of Foreign Wars (VFW), American Legion, Elks Club, Knights of Columbus and others all had family activities, as well as well-stocked bars and things to do involving drinking. There was a place out on Whitesburg Drive called Cameron's Supper Club that used to have all kinds of famous entertainers. Of course, I never was old enough to go there, but I did get to see Brother Dave Gardner, a famous comedian, at the service station down the road just before he went to perform one time. He was one of the most famous entertainers in the '50s, and everyone knew his name then. I understand that he died a pauper in public housing on welfare in Talladega, Alabama. What a shame. Johnny Mathis, Nat King Cole, Dinah Washington and other greats performed at some of the "clubs" in Huntsville back in the '50s.

Teenagers have always had a hard time with substance abuse. Our substance abuse involved drinking and smoking cigarettes. One of our

Beer coolerator.

classmates (name withheld to protect the innocent) made a drink called Purple Passion. I wouldn't want to tell on old Ken for all the tea in China. I remembered consuming some of that one night in the back seat of Scottie's blue 1949 Ford and spilling it all over my white sport coat. I had just had the sport coat rewoven from when someone had flipped a cigarette out the window and burned a hole in the sleeve. Oh, the woes of a teenager.

Those poor soldiers who come into town from Redstone Arsenal on a pass were sitting ducks for the bootleggers and illegal spots. There was a brothel (a nicer way of saying what we called them then) or two where some of the soldiers visited. I empathized with them years later when I was in basic training at Fort Polk, Louisiana.

I am not proud of this, but I remember the first time I ever tasted vodka. We were on a camping trip on a farm on the edge of town, and it was really cold. We didn't have a tent pitched, but we were all huddled up around a big old fire. Someone had the idea to bring some vodka and orange juice. It was all mixed up in a big container and everyone took a swig. I was the last one so I drank what was left in the jug. I didn't drink it, I guzzled it. I don't remember having any trouble sleeping that night, but when I woke up the next morning it was cold. I was not inside my sleeping bag, and my head hurt so bad I felt sick. It was years before I would ever drink orange juice again. I can't even remember tasting vodka again, and today the only thing I want to drink when I am camping is water or coffee. I have a lot of friends who were adversely affected by alcohol.

The Marlboro Man (the cigarette advertisement figure) and the cocktail party in the movies glamorized cigarettes and drinking. I never saw my heroes Gene Autry or Roy Rogers or even John Wayne drinking in any of their movies. They were our heroes and role models. Our teachers were, too. They had to have strict moral conduct. One or two of them slipped through the cracks and fell off the wagon, but everyone knew about it.

Things are a lot different in today's world. Companies quit advertising cigarettes and booze like they used to, and hardly anyone smokes any more compared to those days. Teenagers today seem to know a whole lot more about the ways of the world than we did. The bootleggers aren't gone, they've just changed. The VFW, American Legion and Elks Club are still in business. Oh yeah, I left out the Country Club. I never went to the Country Club except as a guest as a dance date.

The Marlboro Man is reported to have died of cancer, and cigarettes cost so much now that I wonder who could afford the habit.

BOXING AND WRESTLING
IN HUNTSVILLE

"Burt, the boxer, Grady, the raslin' announcer and Coach Grysca"

Burt Gildart transferred to Butler High School in the late '50s. He was a boxer.

Boxing had been a poor boys' sport in Huntsville and not supported by very many people during that period of time. The Boys Club was located in a Quonset hut on Governors Drive, and Mr. Palmer was the director. They had a boxing ring, a pretty nice one. The volunteer instructor/trainer was a man named Buddy. He was good with us boys.

Since it wasn't publicized or glamorized in Huntsville, I am not sure where Burt had all his fights. I assume that he traveled on the Boys Club circuit to Memphis, Nashville, Gadsden, Birmingham and other places. He was a good boxer and we all learned a lot from him. He was a little older than me.

I remember my famous "challenge" fight with Bobby Allen. Bobby was a year older than me and outweighed me. He was also fast with his fists. I was taller and had the reach on him. We wore leather headgear and used sixteen-ounce gloves. You could not really hurt anyone with those gloves. We both were glad when the three rounds were over. Bobby won. He whipped me.

That famous fight got me a reputation at Huntsville High School. Clem Grysca was our football coach and physical education teacher. My first year there, each gym class had to put on boxing gloves and see a demonstration and participate. I thought I was tough. Coach Grysca used me for the demonstration. I can't remember all of the names that I went up against that day, but I do remember how I felt when we were through: beat up but tough.

Boxing seemed to come to an end after one Friday night fight on the Gillette Cavalcade of Sports. There was a match between Benny "Kid" Paret and Emile Griffith on March 24, 1962, at Madison Square Garden in New York, and it was televised live by NBC.

Boxing fans all over the country were glued to their sets. Griffith won the fight. Paret died several days later. Boxing died for a long time after. Muhammad Ali, the boxer; Howard Cosell, the announcer; and all that goes with them brought boxing back to the big time.

If big-time boxing had its Howard Cosell, Huntsville had its Grady Reeves. Reeves was the main announcer at the wrestling matches at the old National Guard Patton Street Armory. He was *the* radio announcer in the '50s. All of us teenagers knew him and listened to him on the air. He would broadcast from the old Holiday House from a glass booth. The location later became known as Boot's Lounge.

When he went on local television and became the sports announcer, the rest was history. He was famous for his fishing reports and people who he had on his show. His morning show was watched by all. I knew Grady from the early days, when he lived over on West Holmes Street. He was a big man with black horn-rimmed glasses and straight black hair. He wasn't afraid to talk to anybody.

For some of the folks in Huntsville, he was one of the best wrestling match ringside announcers around. I was not a major wrestling fan, but we often went with friends. I remember names like Jackie Fargo (I later knew him in Memphis), Gorgeous George, Tex Riley, Dusty Rhodes, Bob Rossi and the Monroe Brothers who went by the names Rocket and Sputnik. But the most famous of all, and the nastiest fighter, was the famous Tojo Yamamoto. Obviously he was from Japan. He always opened with a ceremony that included salt as a prop. Later on he would reach in his trunks, get some of the salt out and throw it in the eyes of his opponent.

The wrestlers were only part of what was going on. Grady Reeves "aiged" everyone on and taunted the wrestlers and the people in the audience. There was always somebody's grandmother or a little old lady who got involved in the match. There were altercations between fans, wrestlers and Grady Reeves. They were all actors. Some pretty good, some pretty bad.

Old-time boxing and wrestling are gone. We had a good time watching it in the '50s. Grady Reeves died and was succeeded by his son Robert, who became as popular as his father. Robert was lucky to be able to grow up working with his dad. Grady went out as everybody's friend and nice man who was good to a lot of people and good at what he did.

Clem Grysca left Huntsville High School to go to the University of Alabama as a coach under the famous Paul "Bear" Bryant. He is still there and is the curator of the Paul "Bear" Bryant Museum in Tuscaloosa, Alabama. Both of these men influenced a lot of people in Huntsville during the 1950s. I was one of them.

I met Jackie Fargo at one of his Memphis restaurants. It was called Fargos, and it was famous for its Fargo Burgers. I remember meeting him real late one night at the cash register. He didn't look so tough to me.

Shades of B. Allen vs. J. Ferguson, 1957.

CAVE EXPLORING
AROUND HUNTSVILLE

"Literally Explorer Scouts"

Being in the Boy Scouts of America in Huntsville during the '50s was a real experience that allowed us to do a lot of things that kids only dream about. One of the things we got to do was go cave exploring.

The first real cave I had ever been in was Luray Caverns in Virginia back in the '40s and a host of others only as a tourist and not as a cave explorer.

The first real exciting cave exploring trip I took was to Cathedral Caverns in 1955 when Mr. Jay Gurley bought it. There was a lot to see and do. We used carbide head lanterns. The caves contain the largest stalagmite in the world and a lot of other unusual things. There was a room we went into that was filled with solid soda straw–type calcium deposits. Evidently we were the first ones to crawl into that area of the cave, because we had to break the stalactite straws out of our way to get into the main room. Today it is part of the Alabama Park System and is quite a tourist attraction.

Other caves included the Salt Peter Cave up in Jackson County and Guntersville Caverns on Highway 79 south of Guntersville near the Sidney community.

We went out to Redstone Arsenal to a manmade entrance to a cavern that was connected to an underground storage for chemicals. The entrance was a test for our group to see if we had it in us to be spelunkers. It was just big enough for a man to go through. It was kind of like crawling through a modern CAT scan machine. You had to hold your hands out in front and

Local speleologists.

drag yourself in using the tips of your toes for motivation. The inside was like a big empty Quonset hut complete with lights and all.

Our scoutmaster had put us to a good test. There were also cave crickets, bats and spiders to contend with. My brother Richard went on this trip, and he had the hardest time getting through. He was a good sport, though, and made it through fine. Even though we are brothers we are not a lot alike, but I will say that we did a lot of things that were adventurous together when we were growing up in Huntsville during the '50s. Of course when we all got into the cave and the scoutmaster gave us his approval, we just simply walked out erect through the main entrance.

Probably the most dangerous caves we went in were the old coal mines on the side of Monte Sano overlooking Huntsville. They were used during the Civil War to mine coal. A miner during the war could haul out over three thousand pounds per day by himself to be hauled off to town on a coal wagon.

The old mining roads were still visible during the '50s, and we used to look for artifacts quite often. We found lots of agates and fossils on those old roads.

Glimpses of Huntsville in the 1950s

Santa Cave, lower passage.

The Huntsville Caverns are out on Pulaski Pike. The entrance was tough. There was a lot of mud to wade through. It was almost waist high. Donnie Morton lost one of his tennis shoes and never looked back to try to retrieve it. Tom Cornell was the scoutmaster who brought the troop in. During prohibition there was a nightclub in the caverns. This was long before my time. Today it is closed to the public.

There was another cave we went in on Monte Sano. We called it the Bottomless Pit. Today they call it the Natural Well. It took over two hundred feet of heavy rope to go down to the big room at the bottom. The room had a one-hundred-foot ceiling, and there was an active waterfall that was about twenty feet high. There were a lot of rumors floating around about the Bottomless Pit and other caves and sinkholes on Monte Sano.

One rumor was that someone had put a bunch of ducks down in one of the holes on top of Monte Sano and they came out at the Big Spring in Huntsville. Another rumor was that someone had put dye in a sinkhole on the Monte Sano Mountain and the water at the Big Spring had turned the color of the dye.

Wayne Short and Gordon Shearer decided to dispel another rumor that was going around. Remember this was the '50s before we had GPS and equipment like we have today with which to find places underground. The rumor was that there was a huge cavern under the Madison County Courthouse. Wayne and Gordon wrapped flashlights in tape to make them waterproof. They put on their swimming trunks (two young Elvis lookalikes) and found just the right time to slip up to the Big Spring and go into the opening.

It was not barricaded or protected at the time. They had to walk with their legs stretched out on each side until they passed into the spot that looked like

Eudy Cave.

a cave entrance. With their flashlights on and assuming their best Tarzan stances, they reached total failure and disappointment. The big crack that looked like the opening to a cave had been completely covered over with mortar.

To this day I have not found any evidence of any dye or ducks being turned loose or put down any sinkholes or caves on Monte Sano and showing up in Huntsville. I did find out that the possibility of a cave being under the courthouse was true. When the city built the courthouse in 1964, they definitely found that there was a cavern under the square. Several local concrete companies won work bids on the concrete for the job. Van Valkenburgh Brothers Concrete Company was one of the companies that won a contract.

My friend and former classmate from Huntsville High School, Richard Van Valkenburgh, a member of the family that owned the firm, was the dispatcher. Their company had won the contract for the underground piers or caissons that would be required. When they went through solid air drilling, they knew they were in the cave that everyone had talked about.

Each caisson was drilled about three feet wide with a bell-shaped bottom and filled with 4,500 pounds per square inch of concrete. They worked around the clock for days filling in the holes that had been drilled. The concrete was extra thick and dryer than standard material. That's why today's courthouse has nine stories on one side and only two on the other side. There is a cave under the courthouse! All this happened right around Huntsville during the '50s. It was an adventurous time for all, especially a young boy full of vim and vigor. We enjoyed spelunking.

By the way, if you want to go into the cave today, you have to enter through a manhole on Greene Street. Better get a permit from the City of Huntsville first or you will be arrested and in deep trouble.

CRAPPIE, BASS, CATFISH
AND BREAM

"Fishin' for meat instead of a trophy."

Bailey's Tackle Shop on Governor's Drive is one of the oldest tackle shops in Huntsville. I remember seeing my first Ambassador casting reel there and my first Quick spinning reel. Both were imported from Sweden at the time. I drooled when I saw the two reels and knew that one day I would have to have one of each.

Mr. Bailey would stand in the door with the Quick spinning outfit and cast a rubber plug in a straight line all the way out to Governor's Drive. He had total control and accuracy, and everyone was excited when he demonstrated his skills.

Fishing and baseball were two of the top activities for most of us boys in the summer. Heck, we would go fishing or play ball at the drop of a hat. During crappie season, we would go to the Tennessee River and load up. Usually the crappie were biting when the dogwood trees started blooming. They were on the bed or spawning.

One of the best-known fishermen in the Huntsville Area during the '50s was Country Bailey. I knew him as a produce customer when I worked at Kroger Grocery. He always had a good fishing story, and I was always glad to listen. I also had the privilege of going fishing with him for crappie and largemouth bass. He took a lot of people fishing.

The most famous fishing personality he took fishing was Gadabout Gaddis. Gaddis had a syndicated fishing program that was filmed for

Tennessee River Group visit.

television and movie theatres. Everyone was excited when he came to Huntsville to film his show. They went to Mud Creek to film the show. It was called *The Flying Fisherman.*

Country Bailey took him to a good spot at the right time because they were catching two at a time. Most people would rather eat crappie than any other fish. I liked catfish better and loved to catch them. Hand grappling, trot-lining or bait casting were the three main methods we used to catch them.

Grappling in the creeks and small rivers like the Flint, Paint and Elk was an exciting way to catch the fish. You wade in the water and stick your hand up under the rocks where the fish were hiding. You had to be careful of a few things like snakes, catfish fins and snapping turtles. All three liked to hide in the same place. All you needed was a little courage and a croaker sack to put them in after you grappled them.

Trot-lining was a lucrative way of catching catfish. Many people made their living running trotlines on the Tennessee River. A trotline was a staging line with a lot of hooks. They were baited with all sorts of things ranging from catawpala worms, Ivory soap, night crawler worms, livers, chicken guts and more. The line was usually tied to a tree on the river bank and stretched out into the river with a weight on the end to hold it down. Most trotline fishermen ran their lines at night or very early in the morning. Sometimes twice a day. It was a lot of work for some and fun for others.

Many restaurants around Huntsville advertised fresh Tennessee River catfish on their menus. The old Greenbriar Restaurant at Greenbriar and later on the Catfish Haven on the south side of the Tennessee River were the best. Today most restaurant catfish are pond raised on catfish farms, a lot of them in Alabama.

Bream fishing was for everybody. Bream were in every pond, creek, rill or run, and just about anyone could catch one if they had a small enough hook, a worm or cricket. We used to catch all we wanted in little ponds around Huntsville and in the creeks. We would bring them home to mom, and she would fry them up for us. It took a lot of them to make a mess for a meal.

In the summer, when the willow flies were hatched out, the bream would hit anything that you threw on top of the water. If you had a fly rod with a cork popping bug, you could have a lot of fun catching them.

Bass fishing was nothing in the '50s like it is today. Today a fish almost has to be a world's record to get a picture of it in the paper. Back in the '50s you could catch a four-pound largemouth bass and get your picture in the *Huntsville Times* with your fish. Every week they had a photo of someone holding a fish. Not as many people were fishing back then, and the equipment was a lot simpler.

Our trolling motor was a boat paddle. I could skull a boat pretty good with a boat paddle along the banks of the Tennessee River. We used to show up at the boat docks during crappie season, and we would "hire out" for the day. Pay was usually one dollar, some of the fish and a ride home. It was a pretty good deal for a boy who liked to fish but had no boat. There was always a sandwich or some "viennas" in the deal, with a Double Cola or "belly washer."

Fishing was something that a lot of folks in the '50s took time out to do. Times were changing, but everybody had a fishing pole. A lot of folks can relate to the tune from *The Andy Griffin Show* on television when they see Andy and little Opie walking down the road together. The background tune being whistled is called "The Fishing Hole."

Crappie, bream, largemouth bass or catfish. Take your pick! Mine's catfish!

FROM DELIVERY BOY
TO PRODUCE CLERK

"The first two jobs I had for a paycheck"

My dad was a professional soldier until he retired, so there was a lot of discipline in our home. He was taught carpentry and cabinetmaking as a boy before going into the army. My two brothers and I learned that from him.

We always had jobs to do at the house or were always working on a project. Dad's motto was: "As long as you put your feet under our table you will follow our rules and do your share. When you start paying your way then you can do different." Now don't get me wrong. We got an allowance—not much, but I now realize that it was what he could afford.

This caused me to be creative and resourceful in ways to make extra money. In the winter, there were leaves and pine straw to be raked. Christmas trees, wreaths and mistletoe to be gathered and sold. Attempts at door-to-door sales with such products as the *Grit* newspaper, Cloverine salve, flower and vegetable seeds, homemade potholders and aprons made by Mom, magazine subscriptions, hickory nuts and walnuts and more. In the spring and summer, the grass started growing and yards needed to be mowed and raked. Folks had not caught on to the gasoline-operated rotary lawnmowers yet, so if you had one you could make some good money. You could even have regular customers.

There were lots of ways to make extra money but nothing you could depend on year round unless you had a regular job. I wanted a regular job but it was hard to find one year round.

Then along came Butch Stevens in a '50s model Volkswagen van. On the side it said ROCKET CITY DELIVERY SERVICE. Butch had gotten himself a job with the first delivery service in Huntsville that would deliver anything. He needed a helper and it paid well. It lasted for the summer and then on through school.

In the morning we went to Corman's donut shop and picked up donuts and pastries to be delivered all over town to the restaurants and places that sold donuts: Burgreen's Cafeteria, the Church Street Sweet Shop, lots of cafés and blue-plate special joints. It was real interesting doing all of that so early in the morning before daylight.

Then we would go to Giles Seed and Feed and pick up a load of items like cow manure, Triple 8 fertilizer, grass seed, bushes, plants, shovels, hoes, rakes—you name it. All of these things were disbursed to the houses in all the new subdivisions. Giles Feed and Seed offered free delivery and we did it.

Then there was the Rexall Drugstore. We delivered the prescription drugs that were called in. It was a great and interesting job. Butch and I had a ball working together. We went to every nook and cranny of Huntsville. There were new addresses and subdivisions opening every week.

There were many other facets to the job that were neat. One of them was the Volkswagen. The engine was located in the rear, and the van could hold quite a bit of stuff. We kept it neat and clean so the pastries and fertilizer would not get mixed up. That job lasted a good part of a summer.

Then I found out that Kroger Grocery on Gallatin Street was looking for a trainee for the produce department. Billy Guest and Bobby Grubbs both worked at Kroger. They were friends of mine. Billy worked in the grocery department and Bobby was a meat cutter.

We all went to Huntsville High School and these were after-school jobs, although Bobby may have been in the industrial education program. Billy ended up being a successful attorney in Chattanooga, and Bobby ended up being a successful restauranteur and club owner in Huntsville.

Bobby's daddy used to have the Becon Hamburgers in Huntsville. At one time they had two locations on the Parkway. Mrs. Guest, Billy Guest and Donnie Morton's grandmother, used to be the hostess at Little Farms on Whitesburg. There are lots of stories about Little Farms.

I reported to Kroger for the interview with Mr. Mickle, the store manager, and Mr. Haney, the produce manager. They told me that the job paid seventy-five cents per hour and that I could work as many hours as I wanted to if they were available. I had to wear a white shirt, a blue Kroger's

Kroger on Clinton Avenue.

tie and a clean white apron every day. I had to have a regular haircut and keep my fingernails clean and cut. My shoes had to be polished—no tennis shoes allowed!

The produce department was huge compared to other stores in town. It had five employees. The Kroger Company was headquartered in Cincinnati and prided itself on its meat and fresh produce. Everything came in fresh on a truck every day. Fresh fruits and vegetables, coconuts and more. It all had to be taken out of the boxes and neatly displayed in the produce coolers. Nothing was pre-priced or prepackaged.

The best part about the job was that when a customer wanted something it had to be weighed and put in a bag by a produce clerk. The price was put on a paper bag with a crayon-type marker. This caused a lot of conversation and relationships to be formed with the customers because it was personal contact.

We won a lot of contests at our store for selling the most oranges or selling the most bananas. Of course the produce manager or store manager got to take the trips that were won, but we got the satisfaction of winning. I will never forget the bananas coming in wooden banana crates. They were right off the boats from Central America, and we always looked for tarantula spiders. Someone had found one before my time, and everyone was repeatedly warned about them.

Every Monday morning an old black man by the name of Dennis delivered fresh watercress from Dennis Watercress Company. Huntsville was (and still may be) the watercress capital of the world. Dennis Watercress Company was located north of Huntsville on the Flint River and shipped the product all over the world. I know for a fact that it was shipped to the Waldorf Astoria Hotel in New York and also to the White House at our nation's capital in Washington, D.C. You don't hear much about watercress these days, but I remember the customers at Kroger buying it to make watercress sandwiches. It must have been a "social thing" because we never had any at our house.

I remember the big knife we had for slicing watermelons and how proficient I was with it.

The worst part of the job was cleaning out the produce coolers every Saturday night. It was a hard and dirty job, and we were always in a hurry because it was Saturday night and we were teenagers.

My mom took a picture of me with my first paycheck from Kroger with my white short-sleeved shirt and blue Kroger tie and Butch wax flat-top haircut. My parents were proud of me, and I ended up working there until I graduated from high school.

After all, seventy-five cents was pretty good money then for a student in high school. Most of all what I remember liking about both jobs was the "people contact": seeing the smiling faces of the people that the Rocket City delivery job put me in front of when I brought them there items and the personal contact with the folks at Kroger when I weighed their produce. Rocket City Delivery is history now, but I still see Butch and we have fun remembering it.

Kroger expanded in Huntsville and moved to other locations, and the old Gallatin Street spot is now part of the hospital complex. To this day I have a special place in my heart for the memories of these two jobs I had in Huntsville before I left home.

HULA-HOOPS, HIFI, YO-YOS AND TELEVISION

"Everybody gets television in Huntsville."

I never could make a Hula-Hoop work for me. The thin, light plastic tube that came in all kinds of colors were quite the rage. Just about everyone got one.

The first Hula-Hoop I saw was at the Parkway City Shopping Center before it was made into a mall. They had Hula-Hoop contests for all ages. Little kids seemed to catch the hang of it better than older folks. I never was very good at doing it and didn't spend a lot of time trying. The Hula-Hoop movement evolved into a feat good enough to become a circus talent act. Some people could twirl several Hula-Hoops at one time.

Parkway City Shopping Center was a new place to go for many of the citizens of Huntsville. It was a brand-new complex. All of the stores had separate exterior entrances, kind of like a big strip mall. Parkway City was a big deal at the end of the '50s.

People watching sort of slacked off as a popular thing to do on the Madison County Courthouse Square, and folks started going to the Parkway City Shopping Center to gawk at one another. Then they made a mall out of it and kept expanding.

Montgomery Wards moved its downtown store from the courthouse square to the shopping center. It was quite a store. Burgreen's Cafeteria was also located there. It was an immediate, huge success. The Parkway City Shopping Center has evolved into the big multilevel center that it is today—quite a long way from a strip mall.

It was and still is one of the centers of activity for folks to gather. People go to the Parkway Mall and other places to do their walking exercises. People of all ages were hula-hooping. You slipped it over your head, gyrated your hips and the plastic tube went around and around. Some people could do two or more of them at once.

Yo-yos were very popular in the '50s in Huntsville. The "yo-yo man" came around to the schools in the early '50s to the playgrounds and after-school hangouts. I think he was Japanese. He sold yo-yos for his income. They cost anywhere from ten cents to one dollar depending on how elaborate you wanted to go. He had a razor-sharp knife and would carve your name with a design on it if you bought one of his wooden yo-yos. He could do all kinds of tricks and manipulate several of them at one time. A little direction book came with one of his yo-yos. When he came to Butler School, he was driving a little Volkswagen car, and it was loaded down with yo-yos. He was cool and got our attention, even though his English wasn't very good. I wonder how he would do today selling yo-yos and how much they might cost? He would not be let on to the school grounds today unless he had a special pass and permit.

In the '50s, anyone could hawk something on the school grounds. I even remember people coming around to the grounds to do pinstriping on cars. They had other decorations they could also put on, like flames and lightning bolts. They used to gather a crowd to show their samples. Most of them guys had greasy hair with ducktail haircuts. It was part of the persona.

I guess music was also a big deal in the '50s. Every place had a jukebox. We had an old 78 rpm combination phonograph/AM radio at home—nothing special but deeply appreciated. My brother Richard and I had notches cut out on the radio dial for all the music and story times we wanted to hear. We would turn it on after everyone went to sleep and get real close so we could hear without waking everyone else up. I liked to listen to New Orleans, St. Louis and Chicago. The jazz and big-band music was always on late at night. I wasn't into rock and roll or old country as some of my friends were at the time. I still have that old radio. No one had heard of stereo yet.

Mom and Dad had their prized records from the big-band era and some children's records from the likes of Arthur Godfrey and Gene Autry Melody Ranch. Otherwise, we had to go to somewhere else to hear the latest on the radio and the latest 45 rpm records.

The first hi-fi I saw was at Roberta Watts's (now Mrs. Burton Case) home on Echols Hill. That home was given to the University of Alabama of Huntsville from the Watts estate. I was in the seventh grade at Huntsville Junior High School when I went to her home. She seemed to have all the cool records, and the kids there that day knew all the latest dances. I never was a good dancer and never did learn how to do the bop and other dances of the day. That's what we called it, the bop.

Sharon Johnson was another friend that had all the records and a hi-fi record player. I rode to school with her in her blue 1955 Ford station wagon. She and her brother Barry had a lot of good get-togethers at their home. Sharon was killed in an airplane accident while in college. They named Sharon Johnson Park in Madison County in her honor. Barry is now a noted sculptor, and his works are shown all over the world. He is based in Baltimore, Maryland.

The Johnson family owned Johnson Concrete Company. They lived in a modern home on the corner of Big Cove Road and Governor's Drive. The portion of Big Cove Road in front of their home was called "upside-down hill." You could stop your car at what looked like the bottom of a hill and it would roll uphill. Of course this was an optical illusion, but everyone in town knew about it and had to try it out.

The music of our day was important to us. Our parents got on to us just as the parents of today chastise their children about their music. "Tutti Frutti, oh Rudy…A whop bop a lu mop…a whop bam boo." I mean, what was wrong with that?

I guess something that had one of the biggest impacts on our life in the '50s was television. You had to have an antenna on top of your house to pick up anything in Huntsville until Mr. Pollard hooked up an antenna to a home a few blocks up the hill from where he lived and ran it to his house. It went to the home of Jimmy and Susie Watts on Echols Hill, Roberta's mom and dad. The rest is history. Cable television had evolved.

By the way, Buster Pollard, the son of the innovative cable man, was a friend of mine all through school. We stayed in touch over the years until he passed away. He had a keen interest in old wooden motorboats. He was always nice to me and was always a good listener. He and his high school sweetheart Ann were made for each other and always looked good on the dance floor.

Pretty soon more people used his cable, which had its tower up on Monte Sano behind the old Burritt home. That was the beginning of Television Distribution System. It was the forerunner of Huntsville Cable Company. Huntsville Cable was one of the first television cable companies in the United States.

Folks got used to television right away, and families were glued to their sets for their favorite programs. *I Love Lucy, Gunsmoke, Bonanza, Sid Caesar* and a host of others kept us all enthralled. A lot of homework from school did not get done because of television. There were a lot of live shows back then. The Gillette Cavalcade of Sports was my favorite show to watch. They always had some exciting sports event that we could only see on television. Boxing was my favorite.

Gadabout Gaddis and his show *The Flying Fisherman* was another one of my favorite shows. He flew all over the United States with his airplane to show some of the most exciting fishing in the country. He was quite a character. I got to meet him when he came to Huntsville to film some crappie fishing shows.

Soap operas began to be popular with housewives. Cartoons and cowboy movies were also very, very popular with the kids. A lot of us teenagers watched Dick Clark and *American Bandstand* to hear the latest tunes and watch the latest dances. All the famous stars were also on the show.

The younger kids watched Benny Carl out of Birmingham with his children's show every day after school. The kids all sat on bleachers and were called the peanut gallery. Benny Carl came to Huntsville to film a show at the Russell Erskine Hotel. He gave away five hundred snap-brim caps. They were made out of foam and had the Birmingham television logo on them. They came in two colors, hot pink and chartreuse green.

Cousin Cliff Holman had a kids show on television out of Birmingham. His first show was *The Tiptop Show* and then his second and most popular was *The Popeye Show*. Everybody loved Benny Carl and Cousin Cliff.

Country Boy Eddie was another show that people watched early in the mornings. His show became an icon in the country music business, and a lot of country music talent was on his show. Huntsville had no local television stations until the early 1960s. Television began to take up a lot of time, and folks devoted their evenings to watching.

Hula-Hoops, yo-yos, music boxes and television were just a slice of the many changes in the '50s in Huntsville. A whop bop a lu mop…a whop bam boo!

MY FIRST FORMAL BANQUET

"How to eat barbecued chicken in public"

I can't remember what kind of formal banquet was my first, but my date was Marie. She asked me to be her date. I had been to several formal events before but never to a banquet with a girl. I'm glad it was Marie because we were good friends. No romance, just good friends. At least on my part.

I had a white sport coat and all the trimmings. I was not bad looking with that outfit, and I had a darn near perfect flat-top haircut complete with Butch wax.

I borrowed Butch Stevens's 1950 Plymouth. It was pink and gray. Marie looked good in her long formal pink gown. I bought her a corsage, and she had gotten me a pink carnation boutonniere.

We road around in Butch's car a while and then went to the Huntsville High School gym for the event. Everyone that had a date was standing around holding hands and looking all grown up. The guys that didn't have a date were all bunched up over in the corner telling tales and staring at everybody. The girls without dates were basically doing the same over in the other corner. Someone gave the signal for us all to sit down in our places.

Marie and I sat down. She was on my right. Across the table sat Sherwood (not her real name) and her date. She had on a beautiful white gown that was very low cut and revealing in the front. Obviously everyone noticed. When you are sixteen years old, you begin to notice even more.

Then after a little chitchat, the food was brought out on carts and served. I had wondered all day what we were going to have to eat. Would it be a

Space Day parade.

steak? Would it be ham? Would it be fried chicken? No, it was barbecued chicken—one half of a barbecued chicken just dripping and oozing with tasty-looking barbecue sauce. There was a baked potato, coleslaw and a roll with butter. We had sweet tea to drink. Yum!

Then someone said the blessing and welcomed everyone. We started to eat. Then it hit me! The only way I had every eaten chicken was with my fingers. I looked around, and everyone was using their knife and fork to eat their chicken. Marie started in on hers, and Sherwood and her date were going to town on theirs.

I was embarrassed. The only thing I knew to do was to mimic what they were all doing. I firmly placed my fork into the inner joint of the chicken thigh and my knife next to it. I firmly pushed forward with the fork and pulled back to my right with the knife.

All at once, to my surprise, the thigh flew into the air and went across the table and landed in the bosom of that beautiful white gown that Sherwood was wearing. Just as she was rising up in horror, the leg of the chicken went down the front of Marie's beautiful pink outfit. The rest of the chicken went all over the front and sleeves of my snazzy white sport coat.

I reached across the table to help Sherwood retrieve the thigh from the front of her dress, and she squarely slapped me back. I turned to help Marie and tried to recover the leg, but as she got up it rolled the rest of the way down her dress to the floor. I had chicken and barbecue sauce all over me and everyone around me. The whole banquet crowd was on its feet laughing and carrying on.

Sherwood and her date stormed out muttering something under their breath about how I had just ruined it all and that they would get me back some day.

Marie and I finally got our composure and my face was still as red as the barbecue sauce. The caterers helped clean us up and the place where we were sitting, and Marie convinced me to sit back down. When asked if I we would like another plate, we both replied that we would just wait for dessert if that was all right.

After the banquet, we got back in the 1950 Plymouth and road around for a while burning up the nineteen-cent-per-gallon gas. I took Marie home, gave her a peck on the cheek and said goodnight. Over the years, we talked about that night, as well as many others and laughed about eating barbecued chicken for the first time in public with a knife and fork.

RICKY AND HIS .22

"Out from the west Texas town of El Paso"

I only knew two people from Texas when I was growing up in Huntsville during the '50s: Ricky Bogel and Jimmy Ellis. I was in the Boy Scouts with them and we ran around together. Jimmy always wore cowboy boots. Hardly anyone we knew had real cowboy boots back then.

I believe they both had moved to Huntsville from El Paso. Rick's family lived on Monte Sano in a unique home. It was built in a factory and delivered to them, and they put it together. It was quite unique during the '50s. I also went to church with Ricky. Jimmy lived a few blocks away from where we lived in Hillandale. We got into a lot of things together that were interesting, as I discuss elsewhere in this book.

Ricky and I loved to go fishing. We used to go to Lady Ann's Lake, just west of Huntsville. It was like entering another world. Spanish moss hung from cypress trees, and the water was crystal clear all the time. It was like a south Georgia or Florida Everglades swamp.

We liked to fish for shellcracker bream. We used crickets or worms and fished with spinner reels and rods. We even used a clear plastic float so it would not scare them. It was also snakey at Lady Ann's Lake. The serpents would hang from the trees just like they did in the movies. They were everywhere. Most of them were harmless water snakes, and we sort of got used to them. Not completely though.

One day Ricky and I were out in a small wooden boat deep in the trees in the middle of Lady Ann's Lake. Our boat bumped a tree as we were paddling along, and a bunch of snakes fell out of the trees into the boat. Ricky grabbed his .22 rifle that he had gotten for Christmas and filled the bottom of the boat full of holes trying to shoot the snakes.

Pretty soon after the snakes all swam off, the boat started sinking. We were still sitting down, and the water was going over the sides. I jumped out and started pulling the boat back in the direction where we put in. It must have been some sight.

As I think about it, I am reminded of Humphrey Bogart in the movie *The African Queen*. I didn't have any leeches on me, but I was all eyes as I swam and tugged and grabbed and pulled that old wooden boat back to the bank. Ricky looked like the big cheese in a jungle movie with his rifle held high out of the water while he sat in a wooden boat full of water.

We got back okay and had a great laugh when we got everything accounted for and felt like it was all over. I told him that he was not much of a shot with that new .22 rifle. We wondered how we were going to patch up the boat.

We built a fire and cooked some fish, and I decided that I need a drink of water. I got up from the fire, took a few steps to the water and squatted down to get a drink from a tin measuring cup that I had brought along. As I raised it to my lips I saw a shadow like a flash following the cup to my mouth, and then I heard a crack sound from the .22 rifle and jumped up.

At my feet lay one of the biggest cottonmouth moccasin snakes I had ever seen. Ricky stood like the Texan he was and softly asked me if that was a good enough shot. We both were shaking in our jeans. Ricky had saved my life with that .22.

On the way home I asked him if I could shoot his rifle. He said I could but that the last shell he had was the one he shot at the cottonmouth.

Hardly anyone ever believed our story, and when we could we would talk about it. When we were reminded about it in a crowd, we would just look at each other and grin. I lost touch with my friend Ricky over the years. He had served in the navy and in Vietnam. I never did get to meet his wife and children. He passed away several years ago from heart failure. Ricky, I will never forget you and the .22, a friend from the west Texas town of El Paso.

RIDING THE RAILS

"I left home on the train."

My first memory of a train ride was when I was a little boy in the '40s. My mother, my brother Richard and I rode the train from Chicago, Illinois, on the Illinois Central to Anna/Jonesboro, Illinois, to my grandfather's little farm. My dad was off fighting in Europe in World War II. He was a sergeant in the U.S. Army and was a professional soldier. I like to think that I remember everything about that trip, but over the years of growing up I heard my mother talk about it so much that I knew a lot.

My love for trains started when I was young, just like it does probably with all little boys. I rode the train a lot in the '50s as a teenager. I didn't own a car, and it didn't cost much to ride. Every time the train would stop at a train station, the "sandwich man" would come aboard to offer his wares. He carried a basket on his arm with wonderful sandwiches and also offered cold drinks like Coca-Cola or 7 Up in the small bottles.

Before I graduated from Huntsville High School in 1960, I had pretty much covered the eastern seaboard on trains. I went out west one time on a great long trip, but it was nothing like skipping around on the Illinois Central and the old Southern Railway. The trip out west was to California. I'll never forget the scenery and the drastic changes. Leaving the pines of Alabama, Mississippi, Louisiana and east Texas for the scrubs, desert, mountains and high country of west Texas, New Mexico, Arizona and California. I imagined myself a cowboy of some sort, as I somehow always happened to

Huntsville Railway Station.

do. The good old green of Alabama is still my favorite, and the Tennessee Valley is still one of the prettiest places in the world.

I thought about being a hobo for a while. I had met some of them along the way. They always had a lot of good stories to tell, but there was always something empty about them. They reminded me of the circus clown hiding behind the makeup. The persona of the hobo was glamorized in the movies and in a lot of fictional writing.

Leroy and I thought we would try our hands at being hobos one time when we decided to board the train for points east. We were thinking about Chattanooga. There are lots of stories about Chattanooga, but this one is about me and Leroy.

Leroy was a big fellow with long, black, greasy Wild Root Cream Oil hair. He wasn't afraid of anything or anybody. Kind of quiet and short on words. We jumped on a boxcar just as it was out of sight of the station master at the Huntsville Depot. It was loaded down with bricks, and there was just enough room to hide in among the pallets. The bricks were all neatly stacked on the pallets and had straw in between and all around them. We rolled on a mile or two and crawled out from our hiding places to have a look-see at what was going on. It was just turning dark, and everyone was starting to turn on their lights.

I began to itch all over, and I asked Leroy if he was itching. He said no, that he was just fine as he stuck his greasy head out from the boxcar to take a look see. I began to scratch because the itching was beginning to get to me. I told Leroy I was about to go crazy. The bricks were full of chiggers or red bugs, and they were eating me up. I don't guess the chiggers bothered him because he had that old oil on him. I told him I had to get off that train and find me some relief. We knew that the train would either stop or slow down in Gurley out on Highway 72. I told Leroy that I was getting off. He agreed, and when the train slowed down we tumbled off on to the graveled rail bed right in the middle of town.

There were some houses not too far from where we got off. I knocked on the front door of the first one we came to with its lights on. Someone yelled from in the back that they were all out on the back porch. We went on around. There was a bunch of fellows sitting around a table playing cards.

I told them that I was eat up with chiggers and about to go crazy. They all laughed at me. The oldest one said not to worry and that he would help me. He went inside and got a pan of water, a small towel and a bar of lye soap. I went over to the outhouse, took all my clothes off and lathered down with the lye soap. That did the trick.

When I got through with all my chigger fighting and was ready to go, I noticed old Leroy was sitting at the table playing cards with the men. They were all drinking out of a Mason jar that they were passing around. They offered me a swallow. I took one and wanted another even though it burned the heck out of my throat. This went on for quite some time.

Needless to say, when we got back on the next available train we were kind of wobbly. What happened between there and the ensuing trip to Chattanooga is another story.

Another time I found myself dreaming that I was a hobo in Corinth, Mississippi. I was coming back to Huntsville on the Illinois Central from Chicago. I had to wait all night in Corinth for the morning train to Huntsville.

Naturally, I didn't have any money for a hotel or motor court (that is what they used to call motels). I found a baggage cart down at the end of the Corinth Depot that was loaded down with boxes for the morning train to Huntsville. I nestled in for a snooze on the side facing away from the station master so he would not be able to spot me. I was asleep before you could count to ten.

Deep into a snoring, drooling slumber of a sleep I felt a jerk on my arm. It was the station master. He wanted to know where I was going and what I was doing sleeping on his baggage cart. I attempted to tell him that I was

A train engine.

just waiting for the morning train to Huntsville and that I was just grabbing a snooze.

He must have thought that I was running away from home or something because he proceeded to lecture to me about the importance of family and home. Some of his words are still in my memory of right and wrong. He invited me to come on in to the depot station house and nap on the waiting room bench in his office.

I couldn't even dream of being a hobo. People were always so nice. The station master even offered me a sandwich and a Double Cola. I left for Huntsville on the morning train with pleasant thoughts about Corinth, Mississippi. I passed through there many times after that and always enjoyed talking to the old station master.

The saddest and longest train ride I ever had was when I left home to go to Washington and New York after graduating from Huntsville High School. Even though I was a paying customer with a meal ticket all the way, I knew that an era was ending for me.

Hap Butler, a man who worked at Redstone Arsenal with my father, brought me to the Huntsville Depot, where I caught the train. My dad was on a government trip out of town and could not take me. I couldn't sleep on that train ride. I wanted to see every sight I could on the way. I somehow knew that I would not be able to ride the trains much longer. This time I had a ticket, and I was a first-class hobo riding the rails of Huntsville.

The heyday of the passenger trains ended with the '50s. I sure miss them. The old Huntsville Depot is now a museum. All the other buildings are gone and so is the old roundhouse. I still listen for the whistle.

TOMMY AND THE WHITE TURKEYS

"Caught in the act"

This is a story (which I am not proud of) about something that one of my buddies did in the '50s in Huntsville. I am, however, proud of the lesson that was learned from it, and I'm telling this story to show that times were different in Huntsville in the '50s. I wasn't one for getting into trouble doing anything illegal like stealing or destroying property. I was always a sucker for a dare, but I kind of knew my limitations. This is a story about one of my buddies that got caught.

I guess he did it to draw attention to himself for some reason. In another story I tell about the red wool socks and how I got caught taking them from Dunnavants. During the '50s, a lot of people moved into town overnight because of the escalation of the space program.

Sometimes I made bad decisions about who I ran around with. Usually you ran around with someone for short periods of time until you got to know them. Then when you got to know them, they might become your friend. Sometimes, adventure was going to a place you had never been before or doing something that you weren't supposed to be doing.

Things like swimming in the city water tank on Russell Hill off Holmes Street (it was dangerous and we could have been killed). Turning over an outhouse on Halloween as a prank (not a nice thing to do). Playing in the steeple at the Church of the Nativity while it was under construction. Swimming at night in the Big Spring Park lagoon without getting caught.

Big Spring Lagoon.

Snagging carp and buffalo in the Big Spring Park at night (no fishing was allowed). Slipping into somebody's fishing lake or pond. Heisting a watermelon or two from a patch of ripe melons (I could run real fast with a watermelon under each arm). Slipping over a fence to pick a peach or apple or two (I got shot at once for this. Well, maybe he just shot in the air, but at night it is the same thing).

One prank that was totally wrong and backfired on the perpetrator was the dare to steal two turkeys from A&M College. Taking an apple or two or a watermelon was one thing, but taking a turkey, well…

I didn't want to be a part of this prank because it was outright stealing, and I knew it was wrong. I tried to talk the boy out of it. He would not listen. He had been dared by another. I stayed back on the edge of this deal and just listened.

A&M had a wonderful agricultural program, and one of the things the college excelled in was raising beautiful, big, plump turkeys. Because A&M was an "all black" college, we didn't know much about what was going on out there. As a mater of fact, we had just discovered the turkey pen when we were taking a shortcut through the edge of the campus.

None of us had ever seen any turkeys before except a wild one or two when we went to Florida or somewhere in south Alabama. There weren't many wild turkeys in Alabama at the time. Same thing with deer. There were very few in north Alabama.

Tommy (not his real name) would slip down the hill just before dark, over a high fence, and "lift" two beautiful, plump, fat turkeys from the turkey pen. Tommy, though he admitted later that he knew nothing about turkeys, said that he was going to catch him a turkey or two and bring them home for Thanksgiving dinner. He said he was a country boy and that his mom knew how to take care of a chicken so she would obviously know how to take care of a turkey.

The plan was for him to slip over the fence, which was made from a thin wire called chicken wire. It was a tall fence supported by two-by-four boards so it was strong and would hold his weight. He was a pretty big fellow for his age. He was going to tie two turkeys together by their legs and sling them over his shoulder to climb out and abscond with the turkeys.

It all sounded like a good plan to him and some of the others. I didn't think so. What about the noise? They decided that he would put a sock over each one of the turkey's heads so that they would be quiet. He thought he had seen or heard about that in the movies.

Night began to come, and lights started going on in buildings. Tommy crept down the hill and found a place to climb the fence away from where most of the turkeys were gathered. He went over with ease. Slowly he walked down to the other end and waited for the turkeys to calm down. He pulled his socks off and his belt.

Quickly, without any trouble, he grabbed one of the turkeys and put a sock over its head. Then he slipped his belt around its legs. Now he had one turkey caught and proceeded to catch another. It was not as easy to catch another one, so he started to chase one. He reached out while on a run to catch another one and managed to grab him by the legs. He decided not to try to put a sock on the other turkey but to just hold on to him real tight and continue on to the fence to climb out.

As he was putting his foot down on the ground from the fence, a bunch of floodlights came on, and he took off running. It was quite a sight watching him under those lights. Every turkey in the pen was screaming (gobbling) bloody murder and scratching and clawing the heck out of Tommy, including the two he had hold of.

Just as he thought he was safe and away from the area, he ran into a brick wall—Dr. Joseph Fanning Drake, PhD, the head man at A&M. Tommy was scared to death. There was Dr. Drake and two campus security guards standing right behind him. We were within hearing distance of what was being said. It wasn't being said in a whisper, either.

Dr. Drake wanted to know who Tommy was, where he came from, who were his parents, was he acting all alone and, most of all, what was he going to do with those two turkeys. By now Tommy looked a sight. He was crying. He was barefooted and covered with turkey poop. He had scratches all over his face, arms, back and legs. He looked rough.

All at once Dr. Drake started laughing. He, Tommy and the two security guards started walking back to the turkey pen. Dr. Drake took the turkeys from Tommy, threw them back over the fence and handed him back his belt and one sock. He dismissed the two security guards.

"Now what am I going to do about this," he said.

He told Tommy he was wrong for doing what he did. Then they went in his office and stayed a long time. Our imaginations were running wild. What was going to happen to him? We waited and waited. Finally, they both came out of the building—Dr. Joseph Fanning Drake, with his hand on Tommy's shoulder. They both got in Dr. Drake's big automobile and drove off.

We didn't know what to think. Our wheels were turning. Hours later, we slipped around to the back of Tommy's house and knocked on his bedroom window. He stuck his head out and told us the whole story. Dr. Drake had lectured him on the value of those turkeys and why they were raising them. He talked about the research and the future of the poultry industry. He told him about the difference between right and wrong. He did everything except turn him over to the police. He told his parents that Tommy was learning about turkeys and that he was sorry that his clothes were in a mess.

I believe I would rather have had a whipping.

Tommy ended up going to visit Dr. Drake several times as part of his payback for what he had done. That was Huntsville in the '50s. I wonder what would have been Tommy's punishment today if he had done something like that. Would he have been arrested?

I don't want to reveal who Tommy really was, but I can tell you that he became a model citizen. Pretty good for a boy who had been caught in the act.

BOY SCOUTING IN HUNTSVILLE IN THE '50S

"Be Prepared" and "Do a good turn daily"

The best time and place to be a Boy Scout was in the '50s in Huntsville. Why? Because we didn't have all the things in the '50s like cellphones, computers, GPS, four-wheelers, off-road vehicles and more. We were heavily influenced by the military and the hardiness of the trained soldier from Redstone Arsenal.

We all wanted to do adventurous things that we had read about in great books and seen in the movies. We had access to a lot of military surplus. We wore our uniforms proudly, marched in local parades and assisted with many local functions. We all knew the Pledge of Allegiance to our national flag, which we always displayed at our meetings or carried with us when we were attending an event. We always had a prayer at any meeting we had.

One of the troops I belonged to was Troop 69 at the Church of the Nativity on Eustis Street. We met in the basement every Tuesday night. We had many different scoutmasters and assistant scoutmasters from all walks of life and circumstance. Three that stand out were Tom Sanford, a professional geologist; Tony Wilmer, who was involved in the oil and service station business; and David Faber, who was involved in the space program. Tom taught us all about rocks, artifacts, geology, maps and geography. Tony took us on a lot of trips in his station wagon. David Faber taught us a lot of scouting skills, but mostly he was just a nice all-around guy. He had a runabout boat and taught us how to water ski. He used to take us to Guntersville Lake and other places on the Tennessee River in his boat, and we would camp out on the riverbank. Lots of fishing, swimming, arrowhead hunting and exploring. I take credit for introducing Mr. Faber's daughter Judy to my friend Butch Stevens. They got married in the early '60s and have been married ever since. Mr. Faber's son, Dennis, was also in our troop. He died in a plane crash while serving in the U.S. Air Force.

We paid our dues, learned our requirements for rank and merit badges and listened to our leaders. We went to Philmont Scout Ranch in Cimarron, Arizona, the National Jamboree at Valley Forge, Pennsylvania, and to a host of Boy Scout camps, conclaves, campfires and camporees. Every Tuesday night we met in the basement of Ridley Hall at the Church of the Nativity.

Evidently a lot of parents were impressed with the leadership we had because we had members from all over the county. Most of the members of our troop did not go to the Episcopal Church. The church provided all of the support in the way of a meeting place, an adult Boy Scout committee and, lots of times, refreshments and transportation. Men who were role models and on the committee from the church were Tom Sanford, Reverend Emile Joffrion, Mr. Robert Ford (Tommy and Beth's dad), Mr. Green (Nancy's dad), Toney Wilmer, my dad John Ferguson, Neal Roberts, George Ferrell (also my Sunday school teacher) and a host of others during the '50s.

Bill Gretsinger was another mentor to us boys and took us on many camping trips. We used to go to Clear Creek, which ran into what is now Smith Lake, and slide down the moss-covered rock on our rear ends and over a twenty-five-foot waterfall. I got caught in a trot fishing line one time. It was loaded with treble hooks, and they got stuck in my back. The pain was terrific, but Bill knew how to get them out very carefully.

These men were all role models for us. They always were nice and would lend a helping hand. There were several high points during my time with Troop 69. When the surveyors staked out the Memorial Parkway from Normal to Whitesburg, we made the hike. I can't remember the exact mileage, but Normal is located on the highway across from A&M College. Of course Whitesburg is out by Haysland Square at the end of what is now Whitesburg Drive. It was quite interesting to walk down through people's backyards, farms and the back side of all the commercial buildings. We stopped, cooked supper and spent the night on the Fleming Farm near the Airport Road. I kept the pictures of this trip for years because it was just after the cotton had been picked and the weather was cool, pretty drab time of the year for a cotton patch. It was a historic trip, though, or at least we thought it was.

Whitesburg was named after the White family. They have been in the Huntsville Area since the formation of the town. There was a fort there

Huntsville Airport.

during the War of 1812/Creek Indian Wars. Webb White, one of the descendents of the original White family, took us dove shooting on White property that was on the river during the '50s. It was a real treat to shoot that many shells on a trip, and the birds were delicious to eat. We camped out on the property many times and cooked the doves on an open fire.

Many of our camping trips were on the side of or atop Monte Sano Mountain. It was not populated except for the top of the mountain. The old coal mines from the 1800s and the old roads that led to them were explored heavily by our troop.

Most of our hikes started from downtown Huntsville at the Church of the Nativity on Eustis Street. The longest hike from the church was to Decatur, about twenty-one miles from Huntsville. There were numerous others that were longer, but we camped along the way.

We always enjoyed the district camporees at Monte Sano State Park. They were held on the site of the old resort hotel that had burned down long ago.

My favorite place to camp was on the top of the southern part of the mountain that gave a dazzling view of Huntsville. The lights were always beautiful at night. On a very clear night you could see Decatur. A real treat

Madison County Fair structure.

was to observe the rocket engine test firing at night at Redstone Arsenal. It was also the best place to lie on your back and observe the moon and stars at night. Even the occasional airplane was a treat to be seen from this location at night. There weren't as many lights back then, and you could really see well at night.

Camp Westmoreland was the assigned Boy Scout camp for Troop 69. We were members of the Tennessee Valley Council. Johnny Becton was one of the council leaders.

My first trip to summer camp was almost a disaster for me. I had a brand-new Ranger six-inch official Boy Scout hunting knife. I had bought a camp moccasin kit and proceeded to put it together. I should have known better, but I was using the knife for a hole punch to lace up the moccasins. It slipped and almost cut off my little finger at the base. It was bleeding badly, and I was taken to the medic at the infirmary. They decided that it was bad enough to have to go to the emergency room in Florence to have it seen after. Eighteen stitches, and I cut the tendon in my finger. I went back to camp but had to leave off a lot of activities.

I ended up hanging out in the camping and cooking merit badge training area. The guy in charge let me help him out enough to where I learned a lot of things required for the badges. I found out I was pretty good. At the end of the week, the guy in charge had to go home, and they made me the unofficial/official merit badge councilor. I had to get my parents' permission and fill out a bunch of forms to be qualified. It ended up being a real treat for me because over the rest of the season at Camp Westmoreland I got to meet Scouts from all over the council. I also earned a lot of merit badges as the sessions progressed.

My favorite time at camp was the campfire on Friday night when the Order of the Arrow put on programs. The Order of the Arrow is responsible for keeping the Native American movement alive in our country, and I still have a lot of respect for what they do. I later became a member of the Order of the Arrow and became a Vigil, which was as high as you could go.

I have lots of stories to tell about Camp Westmoreland. Other boys I can remember from Huntsville who were councilors were Ivan Falkenberry, Robert Womack and Alan Francis, to name a few.

My proudest moment as a member of the Boy Scouts in Huntsville is when I received my Eagle Scout award at the Sunday morning service at the Church of Nativity. Of course the congregation of the church was all there. It was quite an accomplishment for me in my lifetime, and I have carried it with me all my life as such.

I've used my scouting skills in my adult life on a daily basis. The skills helped me survive in the army and on a lot of my travels in this world. The day that I received my Eagle award my whole family and a lot of my friends were there to see me receive the medal. I have never forgotten the motto of an Eagle Scout: "God and Country." My mom was proud of me that day when she pinned it on me in front of all those people.

I think back about how free we were to be ourselves growing up in the '50s in Huntsville and how much the town and area had to offer a young boy like me.

Thank you Huntsville and thanks to my Mom and Dad for allowing me to be free to learn and grow.

THE LAST OF THE MULE WAGONS

"Uncle Mose and the Cypress Stumps"

The courthouse for Madison County, Alabama, is located in Huntsville. When I was a boy, everyone went to the courthouse square on Saturday morning. There were preachers and gospel singers on one side shouting and singing from the steps to those who congregated to listen. There was a string band or country band on the other side on the steps. Some folks were playing a new kind of music called bluegrass. In between there were people hawking their wares or standing around just talking and visiting.

Years before, the square would be neck to neck with wagons pulled by mules and loaded down with cotton. The cotton was bought and sold or traded on Cotton Row on the west side of the square. It was then loaded onto barges and sent down the Big Spring Canal to Triana to be loaded onto the big riverboats, keelboats and barges. This all changed with the addition of trains and trucking and the new methods for growing and harvesting cotton. People basically quit picking cotton by hand at the end of the '50s, and mechanical cotton pickers took over. It was the end of an agricultural era for many people.

Folks still congregated on the Madison County Courthouse Square in Huntsville. One of the most colorful characters on the square in the '50s was Uncle Mose. He had wooly white hair and big pearly white teeth and was as black as any man could be. He had things to sell and lots of customers to buy his wares. His most popular item was a cypress lamp base. He cut the

A cotton market.

cypress knees down on the river and boiled the bark off of them in a big fifty-five-gallon barrel. A hole was drilled in the center, and the shaft for a lamp cord was inserted and readied for the bulb and shade. The town ladies loved them.

When Uncle Mose went to the river and I had a chance, I rode the fourteen miles with him in the mule wagon. The ride was an experience in itself. He could remember the Civil War, slavery, Reconstruction, cowboys, the Spanish-American War, the San Franciso Earthquake, World War I, the Great Depression, World War II, the Korean War (which was going on) and tons of other things about history. I was all ears.

On a hot day, the smells and sounds were prevalent, and I can still remember them today: the occasional smell of a dead skunk and the reaction by the mule. The mule would hesitantly approach the oncoming smell as he trotted along and almost went to a gallop when we passed the worst part.

When we got to the river, we would set up a camp. Usually, we got there real early in the morning because we would start out before daylight. Uncle Mose would not just cut any stump. He said you had to just thin them out and not clean them out. He didn't want the place to look bad when he got through, and he was planning on plenty of them being there in the future. After we cut them and dragged them back to the camp, we would boil a barrel full all at once.

Transfer by boat and train.

While the stumps were boiling we would fish, trap and gather other things, depending on what time of the year it was. Uncle Mose taught me how to catch those catfish and how to set a swamp rabbit snare. Nothing like catfish or fresh rabbit cooked on an open fire. It was an adventurous experience of a lifetime. Sometimes he would let me and Jim, my best friend, both go with him. We had a great time.

The mule wagon ride back was always just as full of stories as the first ride. I once asked Uncle Mose what he remembered about the riverboats coming to Ditto Landing. He told us that Ditto Landing was all hustle and bustle when the steamboats landed. Cotton was floated from upper Madison County down the Flint River, where it joined the Tennessee River near Ditto Landing. Uncle Mose said that the place was "humming" with boats, wagons, mules and people. There were large keelboats, flatboats and paddle-wheelers.

Of all the boats that impressed Uncle Mose, the showboat was it. There were dancing girls, actors, musicians, orators and all kinds of entertainment.

I got all excited when he started talking about the boats, and he reminded me that the boats were not as important as some other things. Like the mule! The mule was used to plow the crops. The mule was used to haul the crops from the field. The mule was used to haul the crops to the riverboats. The mule was used to haul other supplies to the riverboats. The mule was used to haul products from the riverboats into Huntsville and other points. It was the major means of transportation for most everything when the riverboats came to Ditto Landing. Yes sir! Mules were just as important as the steamboats.

But on Saturday morning in the '50s, Uncle Mose was always on the Madison County Courthouse Square selling those lamps, fresh fish, fire starters and more. It is hard to believe today that the square was full of mule wagons and that folks would buy so many cypress stump lamps. Yes, I remember Uncle Mose and the last of the mule wagons.

THE 1950S-WHAT STYLE IS THIS?

"Cool Cats, Daddy-O's, Dungarees and Poodle Skirts"

The desire for a teenager to be in or accepted in the '50s in Huntsville was probably no greater than it is today. We just didn't have as many things to choose from, but we did use our imaginations.

Huntsville was a town that sprung up overnight, and people came from everywhere to work at Redstone Arsenal. The space age was forming, and the old cotton mill town of Huntsville was changing.

The bole weevil changed things for a lot of people. It wiped out a lot of cotton crops and caused folks to move to town and work in the mills or factories. Huntsville was one of the towns that had its share. Several cotton mills, shoe factories and processing plants were located in Huntsville.

Music was a great influence on our culture in Huntsville. Rock and roll and folk music were in their stages of exploding in the '50s, and we were an integral part of it. Country music was strong in our area, and the Grand Ole Opry was still the center of the music world for a lot of people down south.

I would say that Elvis Presley probably had more influence on our styles in the '50s than anyone else. Some girls even wore their hair like Elvis. Butler High School changed its alma mater to "Love Me Tender," a popular Elvis tune. Pegged black pants and pink shirts with black trim were in. Carl Perkins wrote the tune "Blue Suede Shoes" and Elvis made a hit out of it.

Construction of the third courthouse.

Kookie Burns was on a popular television show with his comb and coined the phrase "Kookie, Kookie, lend me your comb." He was always combing his hair.

Garland and Stan Ryan were two of my friends who had moved from Nashville. They were the first ones we saw wearing Levi's jeans with a western low-slung cut. After they came to Huntsville, it seemed like everyone wanted a pair. Garland walked around all the time with a pocket comb and was always keeping his Hollywood hairstyle neatly combed. He used to make fun of me because I liked milk and soda crackers. It's still one of my favorite snacks late at night. When Garland and I get together and talk, we still talk about the comb, the jeans and the soda crackers and milk.

Flat-top haircuts were the in thing, and a lot of teenagers would put streaks of hydrogen peroxide on their hair to bleach it out. Butch wax, a waxy Vaseline-type stick, was used to keep your hair stiff in front.

A pair of black pants with a belt in the back was cool. Girls wore poodle skirts, which were velvety with the silhouette of a poodle on them. Oxfords and bobby socks were for the girls.

"Wash and wear" and "no iron" had not arrived, so everything had to be pressed. Starched and ironed dresses were common on the girls. One thing everyone had in their backyard was a clothesline. Clothes were either washed by hand or in a wringer-type washer. No one had a clothes dryer yet, or at least we didn't know anyone who did. Clothes were usually washed on Monday and put out on the line to dry. Clothespins held the clothes on the line. It was nothing to see a clothesline full of just about every clothing item a family owned that needed washing.

Smoking on the back porch at Butler High School was condoned for boys, but I never saw the girls smoking.

Drivers education was not cool at school for boys, but I took it because there were some pretty girls taking the class. We had a brand-new 1957 four-door Ford from Woody Anderson Ford. I still remind Ruth Gladney Short and her husband Wayne that she was one of the reasons I took drivers ed. Coach Cotton Rogers was the instructor. He was liked by all and was a good role model. Coach Rogers was our basketball coach. He is in the Alabama Sports Hall of Fame. I never got a date with Ruth, but I sure did want one. Too bad Ruth; you missed out. Ha! Not having a car and a lot of money was the biggest obstacle.

The coolest clothing I had was either a pair of white buck shoes or a Kingston Trio shirt. The Kingston Trio made the song "Tom Dooley" famous.

Of course hats were cool. The porkpie and snap brim were cool, as well as a British newsboy hat with a snap on the brim. I did have a pair of pointed-toed Italian loafers with white lightning bolts on the side. I also had a pair of pants with a belt and buckle on the back. It was supposed to be cool. Never could figure that one out.

Some of the new houses being built had a new room called a den for watching television and relaxing. Outdoor toilets sort of disappeared in Huntsville during the '50s. Most of the substandard housing was eliminated. That's a nice way of saying that the slums and shacks were torn down.

Werner von Braun, the rocket scientist, thought that living conditions for a lot of folks in Huntsville were deplorable. His ideas helped improve housing for many people during the '50s. He also helped Walt Disney make movies about space flight.

Charcoal grilling in the backyard became popular.

I ate my first pizza in the basement at Ridley Hall at the Church of Nativity during a Young People's Social. Pizza is everywhere now, but it was scarce in Huntsville in the '50s. The first pizza parlor I remember was Terry's Pizza.

The Memorial Parkway from Normal in northern Huntsville to Whitesburg at Haysland Square was built in the '50s as a bypass around Huntsville. It was not intended to be the main artery of Huntsville. Traffic before the

Wernher Von Braun, MSFC director.

Parkway was bumper-to-bumper a lot of times, and it was right through the center of town right along side the courthouse.

Of course, the construction of the Parkway helped change the culture of Huntsville. Restaurants, shopping centers and other business ventures made the Parkway the main drag in town.

Glimpses of Huntsville in the 1950s

Fourth Madison courthouse.

School dances were held in the gym and were called sock hops. The gym floor was not damaged if we didn't walk on it with shoes. Grady Reeves was a radio announcer and disc jockey. He would broadcast from the top of a restaurant called the Holiday on the Parkway, and all the teenagers would go out and stand around and watch him through a glass enclosure.

The bowling alley became a big dating spot. The Pin Palace and Plamor were the main ones. Jimmy Certain went on to become a professional bowler and became quite well known. He went to Butler High School.

Baseball was also a big deal in the '50s, and Huntsville had its share of good players. I remember a team during the Huntsville sesquicentennial called the Thiokol Wooly Boogers. It was sponsored by Thiokol, a new Huntsville company. They all had beards because of the celebration.

Donnie Mincher was one of the best baseball players during our time who made it in the big leagues. He played for the Minnesota Twins and other big teams and came back home to be involved with the Huntsville Stars.

I remember when they built the new gym at Butler High School. It was a long way from, but in a direct line from, home plate on the baseball field. Donnie could hit one all the way to the gym.

David Weible and his mom and dad were the biggest baseball fans I ever saw. They knew all the stats. David was a good pitcher and played ball at Southern Illinois.

Don Mincher, first baseman.

All of us played tag football and backyard basketball. Huntsville has always produced its share of good football and basketball players.

The old YMCA in downtown Huntsville was a hangout, as well as the Boys Club on Governor's Drive and the West Huntsville YMCA. B.J. Allison was a coach and leader to a lot of us at the YMCA.

Pool was a big deal in the '50s, and the best three players who I knew at the Boys Club were Audrey Roberts, Johnny Futch and Bobby Allen. Bobby died several years ago. I don't know what happened to Johnny Futch. Audrey Roberts is now Andy Roberts, a well-known attorney at law in Huntsville. He played the trombone in the Huntsville High School band.

We all had our styles of clothing and lingo in the '50s, and I'll have to say it was cool. I haven't heard the words "hep-cat," "daddy-o" and "dungaree" or seen any poodle skirts lately, but they're still around in our memories of growing up in Huntsville.

AFTERWORD

"It ain't over 'til it's over!"

Someone asked me when I decided to write this book if I was going to tell all. I asked them what they meant by that. They wanted to know if I was going to tattle on my friends and acquaintances from the '50s and really tell it all.

I told them that not only was I not going to tell all I knew about my friends but that I was also not going to be able to tell all I knew about growing up in the '50s in one book!

I have enjoyed looking back in my memories and turning "old leaves" over. What fun! I want to thank my wife, Shirley, and daughter, Holly, for allowing me to have the time to myself to do this.

I also want to take this opportunity to tell my two brothers Richard and "Bill" that I love them and enjoyed growing up in the '50s with them.

As they say on the river, "I'll see you 'round the bend."

Check out John Ferguson's website at www.riverboatjohn.net.

Visit us at
www.historypress.net

www.ingramcontent.com/pod-product-compliance
Lightning Source LLC
Chambersburg PA
CBHW060812100426
42813CB00004B/1038